Just beneath My Skin

Just Beneath My Skin

Autobiography and Self-Discovery

Patricia Foster

The University of Georgia Press

Athens and London

Published by the University of Georgia Press
Athens, Georgia 30602
© 2004 by Patricia Foster
All rights reserved
Set in Monotype Garamond by Graphic Composition
Printed and bound by Edwards Brothers
The paper in this book meets the guidelines for
permanence and durability of the Committee on
Production Guidelines for Book Longevity of the
Council on Library Resources.

Printed in the United States of America
08 07 06 05 04 C 5 4 3 2 1
08 07 06 05 04 P 5 4 3 2 1

Library of Congress Cataloging-in-Publication Data
Foster, Patricia, 1948–
Just beneath my skin : autobiography and self-discovery /
Patricia Foster.
        p. cm.
ISBN 0-8203-2682-8 (hardcover : alk. paper) —
ISBN 0-8203-2688-7 (pbk. : alk. paper)
1. Foster, Patricia, 1948– 2. Autobiography—Women
authors. 3. Women—Southern States—Conduct of life.
4. Self-realization—United States. 5. College teachers—
United States—Biography. 6. Alabama—Biography.
7. Iowa—Biography. I. Title.
CT275.F6858A3 2004
976.1′063′092—dc22
2004005107

British Library Cataloging-in-Publication Data available

Contents

Acknowledgments

Many of the essays in this collection originally appeared, sometimes in slightly different form, in the following publications:

The Florida Review: "What Planet Are You From?"
Fourth Genre 3, no. 2 (2001), published by Michigan State University Press: "The Intelligent Heart"
The Gettysburg Review: "A Second Look"
The Ohio Review: "Goody-Goody Girls"
Shenandoah: "Skin"
Southern Humanities Review: "My Savage Mind," "The New Royalists"
The Virginia Quarterly Review: "Outside the Hive: A Meditation on Childlessness," "The Last Essay on Southern Identity"
"My Savage Mind" was named a Notable Essay for 2001 in *The Best American Essays 2002* (Houghlin Mifflin, 2002).
"Goody-Goody Girls" was named a Notable Essay for 2000 in *The Best American Essays 2001* (Houghlin Mifflin, 2001).
"The New Royalists" was named a Notable Essay for 1999 in *The Best American Essays 2000* (Houghlin Mifflin, 2000).
"Outside the Hive" was named a Notable Essay for 1996 in *The Best American Essays 1997* (Houghlin Mifflin, 1997).
"A Second Look" won the Mary Roberts Rinehart Award for nonfiction, 1993.

A small portion of "Just beneath My Skin" first appeared in "By the Sea," by Patricia Foster, *Pedagogy* 4, no. 2. Copyright 2004, Duke University Press. All rights reserved. Used with permission of Duke University Press. The quotation on page 76 is from Jill Ker Conway's *When Memory Speaks* (New York: Alfred A. Knopf, 1998), page 6. The quotation on page 159 is from the *Fairhope Courier,* November 8, 1912.

JUST BENEATH MY SKIN

My mother once told me I should be quiet about trouble. "Don't stir yourself up so much," she said in her soft, southern voice. "You take things too hard." I don't remember what prompted this advice, probably some quiet despair in my twenties, something I moaned and groaned about and wouldn't let go. And yet what I do remember is the worry: *Did I take things too hard?* That seems a necessary question, since taking things too hard can be a real pain in the ass, both for yourself and for those around you. We all know people who twist a thought so much it's drip-dry and empty by the time they've wrung it out. Such people are an absolute bore, and when I see them coming, I head in the opposite direction. By contrast, taking things hard—getting passionately involved and obsessed—is a sign of engagement, a proof of absorption with an idea or a desire or a person who puts a certain kink in your stomach. Now, that's another matter entirely, one that suggests you are destined for a life of self-scrutiny and uncertainty and keeping in touch with the life just beneath your skin.

It also means—and I say this with hesitation—that you're probably in for a bit of damage: You'll take revenge on yourself, become disillusioned with people, watch dreams dissolve. You'll probably *be* a pain in the ass. I guess this is my way of saying that my mother was right. I take things too hard, too seriously. I want to stir up too much, want never to be quiet about the things that excite or provoke me. And worse: I want to write about it. Write about my life. The life of a southern girl who ran away from the South but who, deep in her bones, feels the pull of that history, that story.

A love affair, you might say. *Trouble.*

*   *   *

I write this from far away, a small village by the sea. A village where old men in baggy pants fish from the jetty that juts out into the Mediterranean. A village where a sleepy white dog lies languidly in a wooden chair beside my favorite boulangerie. When I look out my window, tiny sailboats ring the canal, a practice run before the thrill of deeper waters. Surfers straddle their boards, waiting anxiously for the next big wave. Gulls caw as they dip toward the sea, then vanish into the sky. It's a village in southern France, a place where I live for six months while teaching women's autobiography at a French university.

"What do you mean *write about our lives?*" my French students ask, looking perplexed and worried when I tell them we will both read and write autobiography. "What can we *say* about ourselves?"

"Anything that interests you," I reply, but of course, this is insufficient, perhaps even false, since what interests you is not really the point. What you say about yourself has to be much more than that. Autobiography, I tell them, draws on what compels you, frightens you, embarrasses you, pushes you head first into black water.

"Writing requires risk," I add, and yet what I want to tell them is this: We carry a double history inside our heads—*what is and what could be; who we are and who we want to be.* Autobiography tries to explain that history, that doubleness, and in the process we try to reconcile the disparity between the two. And yet autobiography itself carries an inevitable doubleness: promising closure while opening wounds, questioning love and the desire for intimacy while exposing the illusions of both. Autobiography engages in truth but depends on the imagination, on the life just beneath the skin, a life that's impressionistic and fragile.

What I don't know how to tell them is a deeper truth: I write autobiography because, quite often, I forget who I am and have to rediscover myself. On such days there's only a thin wall between irrelevance and meaning. Only if I dig deep beneath the skin can I thicken that wall, shore myself up, brick by clumsy brick. On those days writing helps me make some kind of clarity where there's been only a mess of confusion.

After a month of living in France, I walk alone onto the jetty in the early morning air. The wind whips at my light jacket, blows strands of hair in my face. A silky grayness surrounds me, the sky barely separate from the sea. Waves foam just as they hit the rocks, then as suddenly, the foam disappears. It's too early for the fishermen to be here. It's just me, the sea, and my sadness. I feel alien inside my own skin. I feel creepy. The day before I had a fight with my husband in the grocery store and there seemed no rescue, no comfort in sight. Worse, we fought about a bottle of ketchup.

"We don't need that," I said when he picked up the ketchup. We were having hamburgers, and I ate mine plain, just hamburger, lettuce, and bun.

He fingered it, and I could see his mouth tighten. "I want it."

"But you're leaving for America tomorrow, and I'll have all this ketchup."

"That's ridiculous!" he said. "You can't control everything. I want some ketchup," and he flipped the bottle into the cart, then walked away from me.

"Please," I called after him, but he refused to turn around. Only the French shoppers turned to stare.

Of course, that was just the beginning, the entry to a bigger fight, the one about who we were and how we'd gotten this way.

Now that he's left for America, I feel both abandoned and defiant. As I sit down on the rocks, these feelings solidify into a depressive sadness. What worries me isn't just the fight with my husband but that here I am, the envy of my friends, in idyllic France, feeling lost and miserable. I stare at the water and see the next five months stretched out before me with my ketchup. I will be bored and boring and sad. I will be the only person who lives here who has no friends. I will be crawling on my knees toward my husband, begging him to talk to me. "Just talk to me," I'll say. "Speak English, please." The sadness feels dumb and heavy, a weight on my chest.

As I sit there, a thin seam of light edges across the horizon. I watch that seam broaden, thicken. As I watch, an idea pops into my head, an idea that surprises me. I reach for my notebook and write: *I don't have to fight this sadness. I don't have to overcome it. I don't have to change it. All I have to do is notice it, watch it, let it go wherever it needs to go. Because it's mine, mine, mine, and I need everything that's mine.* Suddenly I laugh. I see a fisherman stepping up onto the jetty, his fishing pole tilting in the wind. When I smile and say, "Bonjour," he straightens his pole and smiles back at me. I think about the ketchup. That stupid ketchup!

Much later after I've made up with my husband, I think about writing, about self-discovery. For me, it's a slow walk down the main drag of my contradictions. It's where I see how keenly I can hold opposing thoughts in my head, two spinning tops demanding attention. The self, I realize, is a malleable tool, always loosening its grip, then seizing up in rigor mortis. It's a crazy trickster. A masochistic con artist. I want to slap it, tell it to shape up, settle down. Besides, it's not what I was led to believe in childhood. Back then I thought that once you stepped over that precarious line into adulthood, the self took on definite form, concrete shape.

I remember watching two women just outside the post office in my Alabama town. Pretending to retie my shoe, I eavesdropped as Ina Lipscomb lectured poor Helen Holmes about her husband's drinking. Helen Holmes looked embarrassed, frazzled, and made covert glances toward her car, where her boys were waiting, motioning frantically. They probably wanted to go to the swimming pool and they knew that the old busybody was holding their mama hostage. Not that Ina Lipscomb paid them any mind. She was too busy talking.

As a child I watched these two women and thought they were complete, fully formed. There was Ina Lipscomb, dogmatic and pompous, never without an opinion, while Helen Holmes was a timid though responsible mother who baked beautiful cakes and went to all the little league games with her kids. To my child's mind, this was *all* they were. A set of visible characteristics. It didn't occur to me that much of life is a confrontation with doubt, that every person walks around with an insoluble problem, a heavy sack of loss. That would seem unbearable. Surely when you were an adult, you knew what to do, didn't you?

Now that I'm an adult, I see things differently. I know that hope is precarious and love often elusive. I know that even Ina Lipscomb has days of despair and insecurity and that Helen Holmes can be testy, perhaps a martyr. I know that selfhood isn't a constant state but as fluid and erratic as the tides of the Mediterranean.

You take things too hard.

Of course, of course.

Because that is exactly what a woman must do.

The truth is that often I don't know what I know until I see it revealed on the page. I don't mean that hidden events emerge in the act of writing or there's a sudden recall of memory. Nothing like that. It's that by writing imaginatively, motive and meaning take shape, sneak out into the light to expose themselves, dancing alone in the spotlight. Perhaps it's because writing about the self gives you a point of view.

In a similar way, cultures too must write their autobiographies, must turn on the bright light and engage in a process of self-discovery. Cultures too must ask: Do I take things too hard or, worse, shirk the necessary scrutiny?

Because I come from a particular place—the small-town South, the place I love—it's here that I center my thoughts. Our culture is a storytelling culture, vernacular, anecdotal, humorous, adventurous. We don't suffer fools, though we may act the fool if it will get us a laugh. We adore beauty and color and excitement: Why go home at midnight if there's music left to dance to? Reflection is not our high point; we'd much rather tell a story. Let New York worry.

And yet I want to propose just that: not worry, but reflection, the humble notion of looking deeply at the crossroads of self and history and speaking its meditative truth. Certainly no other region has gone through such dramatic change in the last few decades. No other place in America has been asked so continuously to revise itself, to awaken from its conservative slumber. And who better to look at this awakening than the autobiographer and essayist? Fiction is one way of speaking one's mind. Autobiography is another, one that makes the writer take on the hard fact of herself. And maybe the act of writing turns that fact into a love affair.

Today I stand at my window and watch the storekeepers and restaurateurs sweep the sand from their entryways and patios. Tipped-over chairs are set right. Tables brushed off. Clean tablecloths put on. Yesterday the mistral winds—winds from the north—blew in and the sea was all whitecaps, the palm trees bent and ragged from such force. I was depressed. It took effort just to walk from the parking lot to my class, to push against all that fierceness. But today it's sunny, warm, the wind tamed and gentle. Fishing boats are coming in with the day's catch.

I stand here watching, imagining much more. Three little boys run toward the jetty, racing to see who will get there first. An old man walks in a shuffling gait behind his frisky dog. The water seems to go on forever, but I know that miles and miles away it touches another shore where my husband waits for me. I imagine that when I return to America I'll be different, changed: My hair will be longer, my tread lighter, my head stuffed with new ideas. I imagine that I'll be happy, that I'll have discovered the secret of tenderness, the formula for contentment. I'll be the girl I've always wanted to be: smart and savvy and smooth as candy. *But I'm not this girl, not yet.*

Instead, I close my eyes, letting the sun bathe me, soothe me. Tomorrow it will be cloudy again. If not tomorrow, the next day. In a week or two another storm will come, the sea raging, the wind moaning, the sky shuttered from warmth. In a few months I'll go home, both the same and different. It's the difference that thrills me, makes me want to write, but it's the sameness that tethers me, keeps me company. It is also the thing that keeps me up at night, this same nagging urge that feels different every time, the urge that embarrasses, that stirs, that makes me dig deep beneath the surface of myself, the thing that causes me to ask *Who am I? What am I becoming?*

"Be quiet," I imagine the frightened part of me saying. "Don't make such a fuss." But it's too late for that. Another part is awake and listening. That part says it's time to speak.

INSIDE THE GIRLS' ROOM

For a long time I didn't think I could get out. The girls' room seemed like a locked box, a fortress, a place of despair. It demanded all the things we've read too much about: beauty, perfection, charm, ambition, things that get lumped together as if they're a package deal. In the fifties that often felt like the truth.

Today the girls' room is roomy, diverse. It has more entrances and exits, more automatic doors. The windows open. The air moves. My niece doesn't think twice about traveling alone to Europe or picking up a hammer and building her own shelves. If she sleeps with a boy she loves (or likes), there's no sense of guilt or imminent tragedy. She's simply following up on the biological imperative to find pleasure in love. If she wants a top-ten law school and a six-figure job, no one shakes her head. The girls' room has changed.

And yet in many parts of the country—in barrios and suburbs, in cities and small towns—girls still feel restricted, feel caught in a private hell. Beauty, perfection, charm, and ambition are still sold to us as a requirement of womanhood, a fact of gender, a transaction sweetened only by the new freedom to act, to make money, to go, go, go.

"The promo today is that there should be no more problems for women," a Harvard junior tells me when I'm visiting Cambridge. "But the reality is quite different. Now we have to be everything: smart, pretty, sexual, nurturing, adversarial, playful. It's just too much!"

I nod. There's still trouble in the girls' room.

In these essays I want to take you inside my girls' room. I don't know if what I see will reflect anymore than my own life in the rural South during the fifties, sixties, and seventies. Sometimes that's all a writer can know. My life back then was afflicted—as lives tend to be—with disorder and confusion eased along by wild hope and a foolish pride. What I've tried to do is look at my girls' room with a clear eye, to put my ear to the wall of my mind and listen in. I wish I had a solution to the problems. I wish I had a formula even for myself. But I don't. All I can do is break my own silence, tell my own story. And hope that someone will tell me hers.

A Second Look ─────────────

Today I'm seized with the desire to scrub myself clean, to unhook the past as if it was an article of clothing I could drop casually, irrelevantly to the floor. Such thoughts, I know, are the stuff of wish fulfillment, of early morning daydreams, of depression and defeat. Yet when they brush my life with their silly, leering faces, their depraved sweetness, I want only to escape. I imagine myself jumping out of bed and running like a maniac to the grocery store to buy toothpaste and cleanser. Or shaving my legs smooth as a bone, putting on a fresh spring dress, and deciding on a purpose for my life. If only the past would let go and leave me in peace, I swear I'd be happy, serene. Yet even as I think this, the woodpecker outside my window begins his surgical clacking, a spider crawls up the slick bathroom wall, and I know there is no escape, that the nature of knowledge is tied to the nature of life.

It all started with what I wanted to be and wasn't. I don't want you to think I was limited in that. I had infinite variations. A whole kaleidoscope of models. I wished I could be like Keri, a sleek, tan swimmer with that wake-up-in-the-morning freshness, breasts rippling beneath a man's T-shirt, her straight blonde hair a river of tangles down her back. She'd stand at the stove, waiting for the coffee to perk, and blow her bangs out with short little bursts of air. I used to envy things like that. Simple things. Sexy things. Like me, she'd just left her husband, but she seemed quite pleased about it, almost content, taking up weaving and yoga, her hair knotted in a loose coil while her fingers worked the yarn.

"There are too many places to go to be stuck in a miserable relationship," she explained, "one that ties you down." I thought of myself when she said that, of the trips I made from the bathroom to the kitchen, from the kitchen to the bedroom, from the bedroom to the bathroom and then back to the kitchen. I could see what she meant. Places to go.

Some days I wished I were more like Laura, my nose stuck in a book, the world of get-ahead madness shut out of existence. Laura didn't even know she was pretty, didn't know that with her feet curled under her and her complete absorption in *Mrs. Dalloway,* she formed a picture of intellectual seduction as if she occupied a sacred moment, one forbidden to the rest of us. She wore plain clothes, white tailored blouses that flapped around her loose woolen pants, her purse always scarred, her shoes never polished, a Kleenex stuffed in her bra. She lived, I imagined, for higher things, things like truth and honor, things so important her husband would never leave her, never risk losing that pure, serene gaze. I knew she'd never buy black garters as I'd done, never wear a wig or apply bottom eyelashes with tiny tubes of glue.

Then, of course, there was Willie: wild but with a cache of family money to prop her up. She had no schedule, no purpose, and didn't give a damn what anybody thought about it either. Willie lived on whims, nurturing her streak of hedonism, dyeing her hair platinum and spraying her crotch silver for Christmas. "My own little decoration," she laughed as she danced naked on her balcony to "Can't Get No . . . Satisfaction," twirling sparklers in her hands, her silver bush gyrating to the beat. She posed as a fugitive from small-town southern life. "Get hitched and get stupid," she called it. "I'll die before I do that!"

Though we all lived in the same building in Memphis, Tennessee, in 1972, I never saw these women together but ping-ponged between their apartments, hoping to catch one or the other at home. One day I lay across Willie's bed, grabbing at her slick red satin sheets while she plucked her eyebrows, being very careful to pull only from underneath. To entertain her, I told stories about my life, how I continued to suck my thumb even after marriage, waking each morning with it clamped between my teeth.

"Better that old thumb than nothing," she said, laughing at me over the magnifying mirror. "Listen, there's this new drummer in town who was really gone on me. A fucking hose monster," she grinned, angling the tweezers near the arch of her nose. "He wants to take me to Las Vegas."

"Really?" I said, uncertain whether this was good or bad. Willie talked about men with a carefree scorn as if they were exciting but ridiculous pets meant only for her entertainment. Because of this, I was never quite at ease with her, never quite sure she understood I was stalled between marriage and divorce, terrified of both, walking on tiptoes to maintain my balance. When she went to the bathroom to wash her face, I picked up one of her detective magazines from the heap on the floor. Willie was the only woman I'd ever known who preferred detective fiction and rodeo catalogs to *Mademoiselle*. I tried to imagine myself as Willie, throwing on red parachute pants and a Stones T-shirt, saying whatever came into my mind. But I knew it was no use. The thoughts in my mind were too dark, too confused, like a fistful of barbed wire. Unlike me, Willie went through life as if it was a circus, standing at each event until she became bored, never questioning why she was there. Though my mother would have called her vulgar, I knew suddenly that Willie was an innocent, a mere child dressed up in adult drag.

"I hate Las Vegas," she said, pawing through a load of clothes for her French bra, her feathered earrings. I didn't answer. Instead, I slipped out of her apartment, deciding I was really more like Laura.

"It's open," Laura called when I knocked, so I walked in and made us both a cup of tea, reaching my hand into the greasy water, then scalding two cups clean. Laura seldom washed dishes. They sat stacked in the sink in tepid water, soap bubbles floating around the edge, a gray dishcloth half-submerged in the middle. Yet her books were all neatly arranged in rows, alphabetically filed, all the important sections underlined in red.

Laura stood at the window, staring out at the activity down below in the street. "All these people," she said sadly, sighing, I thought, for the conditions of their lives.

"Yeah, they're on their way to work," I said, knowing that Laura, who was in graduate school and supported by her parents, didn't quite understand people with ordinary, boring jobs like the one I had at Goldsmith's Department Store.

"No, I mean, *look* at them, all these *new* people moving down here, cluttering up our cities, spouting . . . rhetoric!" She snorted. "They're so H and R."

I came to stand beside her at the window, watching the traffic in its hustle and lulls, horns blowing, people descending from buses and carpools, chattering, laughing, bumping into each other in the rush. "What's H and R?" I felt that thrill of curiosity that jerked me out of my humdrum existence.

"Hip and relevant." She snorted again. "They think they know and we don't. They think they have something to teach us . . . all these northern people rushing down here to tell us how it is, how we're *supposed* to be." I wondered why I'd never noticed this before. I knew I wasn't hip and relevant, wasn't one of those new kind of people, but I hadn't noticed them either.

I looked sideways at Laura, but she seemed deeply troubled by what she saw. I stared down into my tea, wondering if her categories weren't too reductive, too easily dismissive. It made me uneasy, trying to stare down into the crowds, to pick out the hip and relevant people from all the others merely hurrying to work.

Quietly, I sipped my tea. I began to think I had more in common with Keri, who was all curiosity and cheer, with places to go.

Early in the winter of 1972, Keri convinced me to take a trip with her to Knoxville to investigate the art program at the University of Tennessee. Snug in Keri's enthusiasm for new things and places, I followed her thick braid as if it was an umbilical cord that might connect me to a more viable life. And there in the art buildings, I gawked at batik hangings, at wood-block prints, at three-dimensional soft sculptures, at women who seemed oblivious to everything but their work. I want that, I thought, adrenaline rushing like a current through my system.

"Let's do it," I crowed all the way back to Memphis, so excited I finished my application before the end of the evening. In the meantime I got my divorce, its force weakened by the hope of a new life, a best friend. That spring when I got my acceptance to the graduate program, I rushed over to Keri's, already imagining us together, our hands smeared with dye, our heads chock full of designs.

Keri was chopping up tofu, making small, neat bundles to soak in soy sauce. "I never applied," Keri said simply after my first gush of news. "I pretended I did, but I didn't. I'm going back to Robert. He's been coming over lately and I think we've worked things out. He's going to build me a kiln." I stared at her bare feet, at the colorful rugs on her floor, at the row of sprouts on her windowsill, and felt that somehow I had failed. I couldn't be like Keri or Laura or Willie. I couldn't be a hippie, an intellectual, or a hedonist. In fact, I felt as if I had no form, no solid casing that surrounded me, holding in my identity. Instead, I was like one of those surrealistic sculptures I'd seen in Knoxville, lacking support and dripping into the landscape of something else in a kind of violent surrender. My dilemma was one of definition and I didn't know the magic solution. I didn't even know where to look. It was, of course, the beginning of a breakdown, a journey so inconsiderate as to shift me back and forth between apathy and self-loathing, sending me roller-coaster fashion down one path before switching gears and thrusting me into the lap of the other.

What I didn't want to be was me.

Three months after I got my acceptance to the University of Tennessee, I moved into a dorm room in Knoxville, a room well equipped for emotional suicide, empty of all feeling, generically furnished. First, I want you to see me, to see a girl who appears normal enough, though there's something slightly askew in the constant looking into mirrors and mirrored surfaces, including the chrome door handles of institutional buildings (which I had to bend over to see myself in). I'm wearing a tank top and jeans, standard uniform on most college campuses during the early seventies, a bandanna on my head. Large, gold hoop earrings dangle from my ears. I'm thin, svelte, older men would say, and I take pleasure in their comments, in the fact that they turn their heads when I walk by. On the surface there's a sense of sex, of motion, but underneath there's a complicated labyrinth, a maze of conflicting rules about what a woman can be.

It would be a long time before I admitted such confusion. During this period I simply wanted to function. To maintain. And this summer I functioned with the help of a pill bottle filled with straight tequila, Cuervo Gold, I kept stashed in my purse. Before Drawing 101, I went into the bathroom and swigged my "little helper," the bitter taste so offensive it made me wince with disgust as I sat on the toilet, hidden from the world. Some days I felt loosened and creative as I drew from the still life, but more often I was too bombed to do more than doodle, creating heads that looked like misshapen watermelons, bowls of fruit that dripped off the table. On such days I cradled the charcoal fondly in my hands, feeling moments of bliss as I meditated on the food I would eat after class and the long catnap in which I could dream myself into a more glorious life, a life in which I had authority and appeal, a life in which I did more than function. In my dreams I was radiant, poised on the threshold of life. It was what we southern girls wanted to be: *radiant beauties.* "Isn't she darlin'?" was the remark I'd heard about others all my life. "Isn't she looking good?" implied one's life was in order, one's priorities in the right place. Beauty was a sign of health and acceptance, a soul at peace. You see, I was born on the cusp of the Feminist Movement and had cut my teeth on Fifties Southern Gentility, a view of the world whose main tenet was "charm."

Now I think of "charm" as the movement that feminism displaced. It only lacked a name back then, though its philosophy was securely entrenched in my everyday life. To me, it meant you were empowered by your sex, by a secret knowledge of the sexual game in which you always held the prize: that ability to enrapture, to hold the soul of another in the palm of your hand. The prize, I believed, gained you a reprieve from loneliness, ending your separateness as the feast of life began to embrace you, lifting you to the very door of love. Yet in this quest, my self was never at rest. Charm demanded persistence, expansion of my talents. It had the anima of a floor show, a bright and sparkling performance in which if I performed well enough I might even forget it was a performance. I was not so naive as to believe that self-consciousness was a part of charm, nor so sophisticated as to see that the point of any true relationship was to strip away the layers of the persona to reveal one's secret self. I was somewhere in the middle, caught between the desire to know more about myself and the desire to be a smooth, lily-white instrument of seduction.

Like many southern girls, I was raised with the idea that seduction was a woman's ultimate strength. When my sister won runner-up in the Speckled Trout Rodeo Queen contest the summer of eleventh grade, we both considered this, rather than her musical talent, her primary status. Now, other girls whispered about her, passed around her picture from the paper, pointing her out at ball games and parades. Even the most backward person could see that being runner-up in a contest and having your picture taken in an evening gown assured you more dates than being on the honor roll. The honors club held a banquet only once a year, a rather stuffy affair in which we wore plain suits or shirtwaist dresses with pearls, our only adornment a pair of black patent leather heels, a ribbon around our ponytails. It was accepted without question that a woman, though assessed constantly by her own sex, was actually defined by men. "God, what a dog!" guys in my class said freely about any woman with a pug face or too broad hips.

Perhaps the most satisfying day of my adolescence was the afternoon the fake bangs my sister and I'd ordered from *Mademoiselle* arrived C.O.D. from New York. Two weeks earlier we'd each clipped a lock of our curly hair and attached it with Scotch tape to a piece of paper so the fake sample would match. Throughout the school year we'd spent hours straightening our hair by rolling it on orange juice cans, an almost impossible way to sleep. Now with the fake bangs—attached with Velcro on one side, a black velvet band on the other—we could eliminate part of our nightly ritual. After trying them on, we declared ourselves instantly chic, assuring each other that we'd been released from the ultimate insult, "Frizzball!"

By the time I arrived at the University of Tennessee, I had gotten my divorce. I no longer owned the fake bangs, no longer believed that ordered hair or winning beauty contests would save me. I knew that I could not copy the life of any of my friends. Instead, each night after class, I went solitarily back to my dorm room and shut the door to my cubicle before removing my bandanna and staring grimly, obsessively, at my thin, thinning hair. The dermatologist at the University Health Center had explained that my curly blonde hair was shedding because of the strong estrogen birth control pill I'd taken for the four years of my marriage. He recommended I stop the pill now that I was no longer married and comb my hair only once a week, washing it every two weeks. I followed his advice with resolution, for I believed in the long climb back to normalcy. I even believed I knew what normalcy was: It was a sense of ease with men, or at least the appearance of ease. At the time I actually believed the appearance of ease would beget its true sister, as if the development was progressive, like passing from fourth grade to fifth. I guess that's akin to believing that knowledge of sin will keep you from sinning, though now I see that knowledge of anything only opens up its complexity. But at this time I existed on a simpler level: I believed if I looked the way everyone else looked, I'd be normal. If I were normal, I'd relax. If I relaxed, conversation would flow from my lips and friends would beat a path to my door. I would become what I had always longed to become: intensely carefree (a kind of contradiction in terms, I see now).

Each night I put the bandanna back on my head before I went out into the hall, then into the bathroom for those nightly duties. Each morning I wore it at the sink as I brushed my teeth, ashamed for anyone to know, to see that I had a problem. I was sure that what I had to conceal—not just my loss of hair, but my impotence in the world—had simply manifested itself in my person and this dreadful sign must be hidden before someone else made the connection. Ugliness, I assumed, was simply the external tag of an internal confusion, a sign of self-disgust. Yet I still manifested enough of the illusions of power to keep my head above water. I was determined to function.

It was during this time that I was asked to create a three-dimensional self-portrait, to define myself in soft sculpture, a task that excited all my senses, my hands itching to comply. Yet when I remember the portrait I constructed, it seems merely ironic that I made a lavender satin creature, a girl with thick lashes and a coy smile, so rich in feminine stereotypes, so hyped with sex and innocence and wish fulfillment that I wonder how I managed to blind myself so completely. I remember this portrait with a kind of foolish fondness, this attempt to create myself anew using the language that was choking me. Perhaps it's typical of the innocent to create the very fantasy that oppresses, and yet the memory is saddening. It reminds me of Ralph Ellison's black narrator in *Invisible Man,* who at the beginning of the novel gives white men a speech on Negro humility as the road to progress. Like that narrator, I eventually learned that to be a dupe has no redemption. The dupe's territory is just another road to hell, for the world is not built on innocence, honesty, or the help of a kind and gentle hand. But perhaps to want so desperately to be part of anything is the first sickness of mankind, a testament to our naked rage and fear of being alone.

*   *   *

During the summer term I occasionally picked up the phone to call Willie, the only one of my three friends who'd stayed in the same apartment building. Willie still kept odd hours, had bleached her hair to a white cotton blonde, and was now living with a singer named Casper, like the friendly ghost. "But he's got a big, gorgeous you know what," she said, then laughed, waiting for my response.

"What?" I asked, complying.

"A big, gorgeous voice, you ninny."

Willie was so full of the old hype, I couldn't tell her what was happening to me, how frightened I was; instead I plied her with questions about Keri and Laura. She told me all about Keri, who was going to have a baby. "She's big as a cow," Willie said. I could imagine Keri with a baby, a little squirmy thing strapped to her back while she bustled around the kitchen barefoot, dyeing yarn on the stove. Keri, I thought, could still function with twins. Laura, it turned out, had just come back from "behind the Iron Curtain."

"She got a big write-up in the *Commercial Appeal* for that stunt," Willie said. "But she didn't meet any men at all. Here she went halfway around the world and all she can talk about are these old women she interviewed for an article or something. Isn't that awful?"

I agreed with her it was.

"So, what's happening to you?" Willie finally asked, but I could imagine her eyes darting to her toenails as she picked at the Ambush Orange polish.

"Nothing really," I said nonchalantly. "Nothing much at all."

After I talked to Willie, I stared hard at myself, taking off all my clothes and facing the mirror. I saw what I already knew to be true: I'd lost or never had the main requirements for a successful female, breasts and hair. My breasts were never big enough to attract attention. My hair so thin you could see my scalp. I thought of them as a chain of being: *Breasts/Seduction/Maternity/Maturity* and *Hair/Seduction/Enthrallment/Ease*. I tried to blame these two things for the war going on inside me, yet I knew that it was deeper still, that these two things were symptoms, deficits, but the THING itself was bigger, more terrible. The THING was something I couldn't name, couldn't get my fingers on; it was a consciousness I wasn't yet ready to perceive. I was still at the amoebic level, lying on the surface of a culture, taking in all its slogans as if the purpose of living was merely to accept what others tell me is true. Besides, at this point I was still functioning; on brighter days I imagined my hair grown back in, my small breasts cozily hidden by fashionable clothes. I was aware that men still fell in love with me, that men were easily duped, but I didn't trust them for this reason. They seemed simply too stupid to see. In fact, I'd lost respect for most men. Though I was aware they held the cards that made me a success or failure, I knew too much about how the illusion worked, how I could act to please them, which had nothing to do with who I was. What frightened me, of course, was the fear that I wouldn't be able to do it well enough, that I wouldn't be able to extract the favors I needed, and thus would fail in the only competition available to me.

Though I understood the ridiculous standards men in the fifties, sixties, and even early seventies set for women, I didn't know how to battle those standards. They seemed as solid as stone, locked in my psyche with a fierce grip, what feminists now call "internal oppression," the acceptance of standards that degrade and belittle you, reducing you to the level at which the standards say you belong.

Soon after Keri's defection that spring in Memphis, I'd begun dating Jay, a man who, on the surface, at least, put those standards aside in his desire to be with me. I met Jay rather whimsically, spying him across the floor at Goldsmith's Department Store, where I unboxed swimsuits and retagged dresses. I watched as he stood at the edge of the shoe department, brooding over his mustache at the flurry of shoppers who wandered through the store, touching and smelling and buying. Though I walked by him constantly, he refused to notice me, not once lifting his eyes from their serious disdain at the crowds swarming the store. Then one Saturday when I was rushing back from lunch, I almost collided with him, my elbow knocking off the top of one of the boxes he carried. "Oh, sorry," I said, stooping to pick it up. When I put it back in place, our eyes met, and in a flash, he reminded me of the German and Czechoslovakian potato farmers who lived near my hometown, something of their old country stoicism buried in his face. "Are you a potato farmer?" I asked. A ridiculous question. Immediately, I blushed.

"Not yet," he said.

"Well, what *are* you?"

He looked down at the stack of boxes in his hand. "A poet," he said, "and a no-good salesman at the moment." Then he smiled.

I laughed. Why not?

After this chance encounter we began meeting for break and lunch and then every night after work, when we drank tequila and lime juice in iced-tea glasses in the park. While late evening fog rolled toward the banks of the Mississippi River, Jay regaled me with stories of his life at the Iowa Writers' Workshop where everybody was busy sacking everybody else's work, then cranking out theories of art while drinking beer on somebody's back porch. "Of course, that was before my decline," he said dryly, looking at the flat stretch of land that ended in the river, "into this hellhole of pious mediocrity."

I knew he meant the South.

Jay talked about literature, culture, and politics, gave me night-long discourses on the genius of Blake, on the illusion of college professors who want to do good. I mention the topics he discussed only because at the time he was critiquing culture, I was poised alone on a precipice of anxiety, wondering if I could ever fit into the culture he felt so free to criticize. Having grown up in a small southern town, a farm town with no pretensions to culture, a place where the highlight of the summer was the water ballet at the local pool and the Speckled Trout Rodeo Queen Contest at Orange Beach, where girls paraded in

bathing suits, I was firmly entrenched in the provincial. I'd never stud-
ied French or Latin, had visited few museums, and hadn't even seen
many movies, while Jay grew up in New York, had already been to a
famous graduate school, and knew exactly what he wanted to do: to
be a poet and a professor. Though these dreams seemed thwarted at
the moment, he never doubted their validity, their worth.

Despite these disparities in our background, I vacillated between
infatuation and ennui, uncertain of my affection, both charmed and
reticent. But this seemed only to goad Jay further.

I remember the day of my twenty-fifth birthday. The minute I got
off work, we rushed in my car toward his apartment, his body a kinetic
sculpture, too wired to be still. His present was the apotheosis of his
dream, magnificence in objective form. I felt the first fluttering of fear,
afraid that my appreciation could never match his expectations. Intuitively, I began to summon up a whirlwind of emotional feeling, to
spin myself past reality to the very peak of delight. I *would* be de-
lighted. I was determined to be. I expected nothing less from myself
than total ecstasy. No matter that it might be artificial. I would please.

At his apartment, he made me wait outside in the dusky, damp hall,
the smell of disinfectant cloying the walls as the humid air swept
through the corridor. To keep me occupied, he gave me a piece of
bubble gum—my only sin, I had told him once—and I chomped on
it, extracting its sweetness with all the avidness of one who would love
to thrive on decay. Finally, from inside, he called, "Okay, close your
eyes and I'll open the door." I held my breath as he led me into the
apartment, the burst of light from the windows flooding my imagination behind my closed eyes. I stopped chewing, holding the gum in
harness in my jaw until he said, "Okay!"

In front of me, hanging rather lopsidedly inside its tall wire stand,
like some elegant orphan rescued from destruction, stood the most
beautiful, the most fragile birdcage I'd ever seen, the entire cage bulging like the most festive piñata, with over three hundred pieces of

bubble gum crammed and exploding between the delicate wires. Fortunes had been dropped inconspicuously into the bunch. Prophetic rumblings. It *was* magnificent. And I was stunned. Stunned by the creativity, by the pleasure on his face, by the golden light flooding past the blinds, sealing me into a moment of exhilaration and pain. How could I not love him? How dare I?

I knew that Jay wanted me to be glorious, to rise like a phoenix from the misery of my confessed past: my marriage and divorce, my schooling and childhood. Often he'd work himself into a frenzy of magical talking, rubbing against me with his spiritually euphoric self as if he was balm to a wound. His concern for me was both touching and frightening, for the more he talked about me, the more I knew it wasn't me he was discovering, wasn't me who inspired him, but his conception of me, which outstripped anything I could ever be or want to become. He would stand, framed by the light, a swatch of blond hair dipping across his face, his arms gesturing wildly, and I knew in an instant that he was alone in defining the territory I should evolve toward. True, he was offering me a bridge, but the bridge was all of his own making: his philosophy, his ideas, all admirable, sensitive, perceptive ideas, yet definitively his own. I would be magnificent with him, he said frequently. I was magnificent. He was magnificent. Together we would be magnificent beyond belief. I saw us twirling madly above the earth, ethereal, erotic, two passionate beings about to burst into flames, and at the same moment, I knew it was earth I longed to touch. Solid ground. Reality. My passion was for digging, unearthing that badly smeared force that was strangling me, while his was for soaring, trembling at the heights.

I wish I could have said to him, "Listen, there's a war going on. Some 'Thing,' some terrible dirty 'Thing' is trying to kill me. That's where magnificence lies. Right there. In finding it." Back then I couldn't have said such words, for I couldn't explain the war. Instead, I stared at his beautiful form, held as if in suspension by the light, and felt a node of fear sprouting from my belly, flowering into submission.

When I left Memphis, Jay covered my car with rose petals, then three months later he followed me to Knoxville, jobless, inspired, he said, just to be with me. He knew about my hair and said, "I mourn it." He waited impatiently for it to start growing again because I refused to let him touch me until it did. I had the mistaken sensibility that if I was so obviously flawed, I could not be worshipped, and it was worship he offered. Actually, even before my hair fell out I was wary of his total acceptance of me because I could never reciprocate with total acceptance of him. I didn't like his skinny legs and the way he talked so much, pummeling me with words, his inflated sense of self irritating my fragile existence.

What I have learned since then is that there is a type of man who wants an ideal to love, yet someone who is slippery, who runs hot and cold. It is interesting to me now that such men offer a love that seems generous, that looks like the love so many women say they crave. Yet it's not. It's merely a different configuration of the same equation of superiority/inferiority. Often such men talk blue streaks around their heroines, assuming that if nothing else works, they'll simply win them by the sheer effort of talk. I learned later that though this type of man wants to exalt and flatter you, he doesn't want to live with you interdependently, trusting your instincts and desires as equally vigorous as his own. Of course, such men need fragile partners, women whose inadequacies absorb them to the exclusion of trust. Without this condition, there is no rescue, no sense that love has cured what nothing else could cure.

But at the time I could not explain all this. I could only shake my head, saying, "No, please don't. I can't." I became very adept at giving him just enough encouragement to keep him off balance while I pursued my imaginary, perfect self.

*   *   *

One day in late October, I'd just finished a silk screen design and stood for a moment at the window, looking out at the carpet of red and gold leaves. I felt oddly pleased watching the wind whip through the nets of bare trees, the sky mottled with fast-moving clouds. When I went to the bathroom to wash my hands, I glanced quickly in the mirror and was surprised to see a rash of bumps on my chin and left cheek. Bright red and pebbly, they were grouped in clusters like ant bites that marked my face. Certain that this was some allergic reaction to the dyes and paints I'd been using, I rushed to the dermatologist, hoping a simple shot or a week of antibiotics would cure me. In my innocence I trusted that fate wouldn't be so cruel as to give me yet another thing to worry about. Thus, when the doctor pronounced acne—the word hitting me with the force of a bullet—when he stated that it was a response to *going off the strong estrogen pill,* I didn't catch the irony at first. I was too stunned by the diagnosis.

"It'll take six months to a year to clear up," he said pragmatically as if he was predicting the weather. "You've got that sensitive kind of skin."

As the acne progressed—the antibiotics seemed to have no effect—I felt as if my "self" had left my body, that it was paused just beyond me, waiting for a reason to return. I saw myself as split in two, the person outside me, the real self (complete with dreams), could not function in such conflict and had simply decided to pack up and take a vacation since it had lost all sense of power in the world. The self I inhabited was an impostor—temporary and deficient—and with this self, I grappled with school, with art history papers and design projects and the business of living. I lived in shame, yet I became tolerant of this shame since I believed it was ephemeral. I lived only for the future when I could be "me" again, when I could perceive myself as sexually desirable. I was able to live this myth until one morning when I stepped out into the sunlight, the shimmery haze surrounding me like a shield, and the thought struck me, *Maybe this is your real life.*

* * *

Despite my own inner uncertainty, Jay remained loyal, persistent, calling frequently, though I seldom answered. How could I tell him that the person he loved had exited and was no longer in residence? I didn't know the metaphors to use. I couldn't find the words to speak the truth. I simply told him I needed to be alone, that things were rotten and I didn't want to talk. Though at first, he complained, then seemed sorry and hurt, he finally appeared to accept this decision. Yet near Thanksgiving, he called one Friday night around nine, pleading with me to meet him and mutual friends at a bar. I agreed to go. That night I washed my hair and left off the bandanna. Dressed in tight black pants and a long cape of a sweater, I imagined myself as Parisian, a younger, more sexy Anais Nin. When I surveyed myself in the dim mirror—about the same dusky light as a bar—I was almost satisfied with my reflection.

I knew from his face I excited him. He wanted me near, wanted to touch me, to talk and dream. After one drink, in fact, he pleaded with me to go home with him, already holding my hand. After two shots of tequila, he said if I didn't go he'd drink ten straight shots in a row. He meant it seriously, his tendency always toward the melodramatic.

I ordered another glass of wine. "Don't be silly," I said, smiling at him, pretending it was all whimsy.

"I'm not." He withdrew his hand, looked seriously at me. "If you don't come, it'll be you who's being silly."

I looked away from him into the shadows of the smoky bar. Had I felt "normal" I would have gone with him, but now I couldn't risk revealing myself, being vulnerable, open, a damaged soul. I felt bound to the ugliness of my self, but I couldn't bear to have someone else see it, really *see* it. If Jay saw me, his face might show disgust or, perhaps worse, pity and remorse. The thought of either so frightened me, I watched stoically as the row of tequila glasses strung out before him in a soldierly line.

"There," he said, setting down the last. "You win."

But each glass only represented a stage of my own impotence. That night I went home alone.

By this time I had become so confused I knew I would have to leave school. I got permission to finish my semester's work early, and a week later I drove home to Alabama.

In the South during the late sixties and early seventies, it was still considered proper for a young woman to return to the family fold after divorce or disaster. "Don't you want to come home," my mother had asked eight months earlier, "so we can help you get over this thing?" It was believed that with the support of her family, a woman could recover enough of her self-respect to reenter the world, perhaps even search for another man. "Zipper fever," my friends and I used to call it, emphasizing, of course, the man-hunting instincts of the healthy southern belle. While at home the daughter could take her place once again as a dependent child, perhaps substitute teaching for the local school system or doing charity work—organizing bake sales for missionaries in Peru or hosting the Women's Aid Society—for the church. Such activities might have been possible had I come home immediately following my divorce. As it was, I sneaked home like a thief, entering my parents' home and my girlhood bed with relief and fury.

Alone in my cocoon, I recovered my fantasies. I imagined myself six months down the road as a marvelously eccentric artist, reentering the world like some ragman's horse bearing silks. Yet such inflated fantasies alternated with more realistic ones. After looking obsessively at my reflection in a magnifying mirror, I'd prop myself up on pillows and swear to the gods of fate that I'd no longer seek beauty as the prize if only they'd let me be average. Average became my talisman, my goal. Average meant a scattering of pimples, a ducktail's worth of hair. Average was workable, a compromise with the powers of desire. Although it implied the possibility of living the life of a sexless old maid, someone who was unobtrusive and inconspicuous, it meant I could survive in the world. Everywhere I went, I began to look at women on street corners, picking out average-looking women as my models, imagining myself inhabiting a simple life, never flirting, taking out my cheese sandwich at my desk and eating carefully, never leaving the crust.

While at my parents' home, I settled into a routine of sleeping, reading, and visiting the dermatologist. Each evening I took quaaludes—they weren't considered sex drugs in small-town Alabama, but merely tranquilizing pills that could assure a good night's sleep. Most important, they swung me into my new life: *forget, forget.* Only occasionally would I remember Jay. Then I'd take another quaalude, slipping into that sweet psychic syrup the pills induced, and dial his number.

"Bug," he'd say, the old rich desire creeping into his voice. "God, is that you, Bug?" Ever since I'd asked if he grew potatoes, he'd called me Potato Bug, then just Bug.

"Sure," I said. "It's me. It's always me." And we'd fall somehow into a little bit of love talk, a little bit of fantasy making with plans to get together the next month in Knoxville; afterward I'd crawl back into bed, cringing at the phoniness, the pretense. I knew I wasn't going anywhere anytime soon.

To my surprise, relief came from my dermatologist. Dr. Sanders was a short, nondescript man in his early fifties who had recently become interested in art. The first day I went to his office, he scanned my chart, made a quick survey of my face, then said, "So, tell me what you're working on." While he mashed zits, using an odd metal tool that left blood and bruises on my skin, he talked to me about the "pots he threw," and a raku pottery workshop he'd attended at a local college. And always he asked my opinion, was curious about the work I'd done at the university. Cautiously, I began to look forward to these visits, surprised each week that it was my mind, not my body, that brought pleasure.

At home our lives followed my father's demands and desires as if that was the natural course of things, my mother and I orbiting my father's sun, circling and circling like faithful moons.

"A cup of coffee," my father said, looking up from his paper at breakfast. And my mother jumped up to refill his cup.

I sat between them with a pile of eggs on my plate, staring at neither of my parents, ashamed but having no words to express my sorrow.

"Now, don't worry about—" my mother began, leaning toward me, guessing at my troubles.

"Cream," my father said, not looking up. Without a moment's hesitation, my mother got up to fetch the half-and-half. Whatever she'd meant to say to me was left dangling in the air.

I knew she did everything for him, even ironed his underwear and carried his suitcases, and now I did this too: folding his handkerchiefs, matching his socks. And yet at breakfast, my mother was robust and energetic, scrambling eggs, making pancakes.

At night she stood in my doorway in her nightgown and slippers, her face clean of makeup, her hand on the knob. Now she looked more like my mother, smart and sympathetic, less a lady, more a woman in trouble herself. "Things will get better," she said, twisting the tie on her robe. She seemed distracted, uneasy.

"Really?" I sat on my bed, a pile of books on the covers. "How do you know?"

"Because you're taking the medication, doing what the doctor says."

I picked up one of my books, flipped through the pages. "Do you love Daddy?" I asked, surprising myself. I didn't know where this came from. I hadn't been thinking about them.

"Why yes," she said. Then she stopped fiddling with the ties on her robe and stood very still. "But he doesn't see me. He doesn't—" She didn't say anymore, only looked beyond me at the pale blue curtains that hung thick and heavy against the night. "I have to lose a few pounds," she said suddenly, though she'd always been voluptuous but trim, had never had to diet. "You never know what a few pounds can do."

"*Mother.*"

She sighed, leaned against the door. "Well, try to get some sleep, honey. This will all be over with soon."

Though I longed to have faith in her prediction, to see myself soar beyond adversity's reach, I knew in my heart that the antecedent of "this" included not only the ugliness of my body but that unacknowledged fear that lay buried inside me like a seed.

Unlike my mother's gentle prodding, my father's attitude thundered with directness: You were either a credit to the community or you weren't. Those were his terms, and I knew into which category I fit. With him I felt vulnerable and defeated, his judgment resting like a club over my head. As a result, I walked silently around him, leaving wide paths, barely daring to breathe. "You could at least be sociable," he said once, utterly confounded by my failure to succeed. My family never talked about what was happening to me, each of us accepting the deceit that all I needed was a "rest," afraid to mention what might really be at stake. "No one can see me," I scrawled in my journal one night. "Not even myself." What I couldn't see, of course, was that my ideal was a monster that kept me tied like a dog to a post. I was Dr. Jekyll waiting to become the beautiful Mrs. Hyde, even though the transformation might kill me. Having been taught by my culture and family that this was my destiny, I felt mentally paralyzed. Only much later did I realize that such needs, driven deep into the psyche, are difficult to betray, for betrayal requires anger, a weapon forbidden to the woman who must charm.

Yet in a circuitous way, I began to act out a mock rebellion against my fate. Each day I dressed entirely in blue: blue bandanna, turtleneck sweater, belt, pants, and shoes. I imagined myself as a blue pencil striding across an empty page at a swift, almost militant pace. Why this metaphor emerged, I have no clue, yet it implies a new possibility: Having lost access to the feminine, I imaginatively inscribed myself into the masculine as if only then might I act in the world. Though my world was constricted to the size of my room, after that first month's hibernation, I began to scribble notes and designs in my journal until by the third month I became so suffocated with myself, there was nothing left to do but burst out of this cage.

Though I'd originally attended Vanderbilt University and had received my BA, I'd always relied on my blondeness, my animated face and voice, to "get me a job." Now I believed I had nothing but the few textile pieces I'd finished at the University of Tennessee. I had no aesthetic sense of the work, only the realization that I'd made it with the same intense yearning for perfection with which I'd tried to shape myself. Of course, the pieces had refused such a scam, the last three emerging primitive and wild as if the horror of my body had transcribed itself through paint. Yet to my surprise, a local artist, my mother's friend, selected these three. "We can do something with these," she said, and off we went to a nearby shrimping village to photograph the work: a silk screen ogee print furled like a flag from a shrimp boat, a woven rocklike sculpture thrown into a heap of Spanish moss, a reverse-dye circular icon, unevenly formed and heavily stitched with thick black thread, tacked to an old oak tree.

It seems only another irony that I would send these photographs to the design department of Neiman Marcus in Atlanta in hopes of becoming a part of their display department. Yet what more fitting role than that I should dress windows, creating the illusion of perfection for other women to buy? Of course, even applying I'd felt like a phony. I'd had less than a year of art classes, one semester of which I'd been frequently drunk. But send them off I did, and in two weeks went for an interview, the result of which was that I would live in the heavy air of sales while waiting for an opening in design.

It's difficult for me to describe leaving home. Coming back had been like whiplash, hurling me into a fragmented collision with my past. Leaving was no less anguished. I remember almost nothing about that last day, except that it was March and the azaleas were in bloom, the air fresh with that salty moistness that coats the skin, the sun shadowy white at noon. I'm sure that I had lunch and supper with my parents and talked about peripheral things—my room in Atlanta, the packing of my clothes, what bank I would use. What stands out from such generality is only one moment, yet it is a moment that has replayed itself several times in my life, a moment so encapsulated with pain it makes me weak with terror and sympathy.

In all respects, it seems a simple moment: A girl stands before her bathroom mirror, peering at her face as if it is more than skin and bones and hair, as if it holds a precious secret, one that only fate can reveal. The girl stares intensely, hoping that from this reflective surface she'll see to a place so pure it will be like parting the veil. Only then, she believes, will she know what she needs to know. Perhaps I did see clearly that night, for at that moment I knew that I could never change the world through my ability to charm. I don't know what could have initiated this thought except for my humble belief that vision often comes through suffering, as if the sufferer, having fallen through the net of her own complicity, reaches the naked truth. I saw my parents' worried faces float before me, my mother crying as she said, "Make yourself happy," while my father merely waved, seeming utterly confused. I had no idea how to make myself happy and felt only tremendous guilt that I'd failed to become what they'd expected me to become. I burst into tears, my body now stripped of its hope, contracting in pain. Yet I think that I was crying not against my own nature, but against what my nature was expected to become, what I couldn't become. I believe I was crying out my refusal to charm. For that moment, I felt a sense of peace as if I'd burped out an alien force, as if I'd been born whole, new and unshaped. I stared hard at my red eyes, my swollen nose, my puffy face, and knew that I had just killed the monster. Mrs. Hyde was dead, dead, dead. And yet I felt an icy flood of fear, for to make her stay dead was another matter. It meant starting here, from scratch. It meant walking out of this house without the familiar props of the past to hold me up. I began to tremble. I didn't know if I had the strength. The only hope I had was that tonight I'd smashed her. Tonight, she was dead.

When at last I began to breathe easier, I looked beyond my image in the mirror to the world outside my window. I saw the limbs of an old oak tree swagged beneath a heap of Spanish moss, swaying gently in the breeze. I remembered reading somewhere that the moss was a rootless parasite that would eventually kill the tree, yet as the pale sky began to darken, I stood silently staring at the tree until shadows lengthened its lines and the moss became almost indistinguishable from the branches of the tree. In the dusky light, I thought it beautiful.

Recently, I took a walk with a friend who had had cervical cancer in her early thirties. As we walked beneath the live oaks surrounding my house, admiring the swags of Spanish moss and the blooming dogwoods, my friend, to my surprise, began to talk about her regret at not having children. "It's probably unseemly at my age, but I still want them," she said. "Oh, I know I shouldn't get pregnant, but I admit I've toyed with the idea. You see, I can already imagine the baby."

I nodded as if in agreement, though my own mind went dumb with a different anxiety. Although I was also childless, my imagination dug in its heels at the thought of having children. I had no nightmares or dreams about children, as if I'd wandered witlessly into female adulthood without any thought to biology. I felt suddenly uneasy, as if there was something wrong with me, some failure of the imagination, some narrative block. And I say imagination, not body, because having a child is surely as much an act of the imagination as it is of the body. And yet with me, no scenarios spun out their fine threads of possibility. When I tried to see the swirling dot that is a beginning cell, it metamorphosed into a period, that all too familiar symbol of punctuation.

After we had finished our walk and my friend left to meet her husband, I sat alone in my living room, saying softly to myself, *You've got to think about this, you've really got to think.* I realized I'd never come to terms with this fact of childlessness, had never articulated my own private response to it. It seemed to me that I didn't so much make a decision to remain childless as that I woke up at age forty-five and noticed it. Yet I knew this couldn't be true, and I was suddenly curious about the underpinnings of my choice, one unacknowledged by me for a long time.

It began, I think, in history. Not just the history of my family but the history of a region, of a period of American life, the fifties and sixties, when men and women conformed to roles that separated them into neatly ordered camps. For white people, this period was a romanticized version of Eden, when families were generally intact and the economy was bursting at the seams. Every day, middle-class men went out in the world to make a living while their wives stayed home and raised the family, cooking, cleaning and running errands, reading to children and helping them with their homework. On the surface it seemed quite clear which group I should align myself with. And yet I might as well confess it: For most of my life I haven't wanted to be a woman. Or, perhaps, what I feel is much more subversive: I haven't thought of myself as a woman, though goodness knows I've certainly tried all the masks of femininity the market produces. Instead, growing up, I thought of myself as an "it," a neuter, neither phallic nor fecund, neither girl-child nor boy-child. As a teenager I dreamed about becoming a woman the way American writers dream of the pastoral. I felt both the need to return to the feminine and the impossibility of the act.

Of course, such gender ambiguity is probably quite natural, given that in my family, my sister and I were brought up as honorary sons, ambitious boys hiding out in dresses, our long hair a mere frill of affection. "The girls," we were called, and I thought this a sly, preposterous trick. We lived our entire childhood and adolescence in a small southern town, a traditional town in which young girls went off to college, fell in love, got married, had children, and then settled down to a scheduled domesticity: making costumes for dance recitals, hosting fish fries and bake sales for the church, attending little league ball games, sometimes even catching a foul ball. All of this seemed proper and right for the women in our town, and yet my sister and I suspected that we were not meant to repeat such lives.

But how were we to live? Secretly, we imagined ourselves living in some sort of dream city, the two of us hurrying down crowded streets, meeting eccentric people, doing something noteworthy, something that made the hustle and bustle of the world come to a sudden, surprising halt. *The big pond,* my father called it. It sounded so heady, so exciting, we both felt harnessed to ambition as if it was an engine carried buglike on our backs, its motor always running. "Compete, compete, compete," the motor hummed, little hammers beating against our skulls. And yet, miraculously, we were also expected to present ourselves as girls, to be polite, pretty, and accommodating in the social world while the engine revved privately, internally, gearing up for school and competition.

From an early age my sister told me constantly what she intended to do when she grew up: At age ten, after she'd seen Audrey Hepburn in *The Nun's Story,* she wanted to be a religious savior. "I'm going to India and work with the untouchables," she said one night while we were getting ready for bed. "Or maybe with the lepers. I'll put the softest, sweetest smelling Kleenex to the place where their noses used to be."

I listened, partly awed, partly disgusted. "Won't you be scared?"

"Yes," she said, her eyes glazing a little with the thought, "but I'll just have to do it."

At age twelve, after a successful piano performance, the applause convinced her to become a concert pianist. She had strong fingers, an excellent memory, and though she hated to practice on those long, slow summer afternoons when Elizabeth Bennett demanded her attention, she always did well at recitals, which suggested a sure thing. Yet by age fourteen she was accompanying my father to the hospital, looking at blood samples, visiting patients, reading X-rays with him, and it seemed clear that she'd follow in my father's medical footsteps.

Unlike my sister, I was much less successful as an honorary son. I seemed more adept at the feminine pursuits—dance and literature—

which in a small town didn't suggest any career choices at all. Of course, you could be a teacher, but that had little sting. *Anybody* could be a teacher. "You can be a Dixie Darling," my mother said one night during halftime at a football game as we watched them strut across the field, but I turned up my nose. Being a majorette wouldn't hold water to my own missionary zeal, for I believed I should dance with the Joffrey Ballet or the Rockettes at Rockefeller Center. In our family there was no distinction between the two, not even that ballet was high art and the Rockettes mere commercial entertainment. What counted was that they were both public performances in New York City, something you could point to as a decided leap out of the small pond of rural Alabama life. The other alternative was to become Miss America, to win a scholarship and learn what my mother called "poise."

While ambition swam through my bloodstream like a virus, the truth is, I never understood how to direct it, how to get lost to my own curiosity. As a result, I was always in limbo, starting and stopping, obsessing, then quitting, never knowing where to concentrate my energies. One minute I'd be practicing tour jetés, the next doing stunts on my bike, riding through ditches full of kudzu, my arms waving out to the side, the next listening to vocabulary records, repeating *adjudicate, anomaly, attrition, avionics.* I often felt caught like a fish on a hook, wiggling against an inevitable paradox: how to pursue ambition while retaining feminine beauty and charm.

It all made me very tired.

Even as early as age six, I understood that babies changed a woman's life forever. In first grade I remember overhearing a woman say casually to my mother about a pregnant high school girl in our town, "Now her life is over!" I imagined that the young girl and her baby would live the rest of their lives inside a closet or consigned to a cellar with rotting apples and belching furnaces, never to come out for homemade ice cream or for the Lineville Christmas play at the First Methodist Church.

At this time I was enthralled by the lives of older girls, high school girls—particularly those who my parents indicated would "go somewhere in the world"—hoping, I suppose, to follow the arc of their lives. One of my father's friends, Ronnie Flanagan, had such a daughter, Mary Alice, who pranced before us with the sassiness of a woman on the cusp of the world. When we visited their house, I loved to go into Mary Alice's room and watch her sitting at her vanity, rolling her hair on twisted plastic rollers, part of a home permanent kit, pictures of Elvis Presley and Teddy Roosevelt pasted side by side on her mirror. I admired everything about her, from her sharp bossiness with her parents—she argued constantly for an extended curfew, for the right to go to the dances in Pell City, for the right to stay up late and read—to the articulate symmetry of her room, the vanity, the desk, the bookcase, and especially the bed with the crocheted doll dead center, its skirt spread out in a perfect circle. Mary Alice, who was ambitious and decisive, who made A's on all her quizzes, who carried the C–D encyclopedia with her to the bathroom, had a tall handsome boyfriend, Mitchell, who was as shy as she was talkative. When he came to pick her up, his beauty seemed to fade a little before the force of her personality, and yet Mary Alice always touched his shirt affectionately and beamed a trigger-happy smile. Mitchell had a younger brother who was in my class, a boy named Peter who did swashbuckling tricks with a stick to impress the girls.

Unlike Mary Alice, Mrs. Flanagan was nervous and jittery, all her attention tied to cleaning up the bathroom and kitchen and sewing Mary Alice's next prom dress with tiers of blue ruffles and a flounce at the scooped neck like the dresses on the antebellum girls on the calendars she ordered from J.C. Penny. Mary Alice was always saying, "Mother, don't *worry* about it," as if she was the adult and her mother the anxious child.

It happened that in the fall of my first grade year I became enamored with Peter, and it was agreed between us in our carefully worded notes that we would be boyfriend and girlfriend for the year, with occasional heated hand holding in the cloakroom. It pleased me to be chosen by someone who was connected, even incidentally, to Mary Alice. Peter said she ate dinner with his family every week, that one time he caught her smoking a cigarette in the backyard and when she saw him, she pitched the cigarette across the street into the ditch and asked him if he could throw that far. He said of course he could and threw his mother's garden trowel into the next field.

Near Thanksgiving, the weather turned slightly cooler so that we had to wear jackets over our dresses, and knee socks instead of the short, folded down kind we'd been wearing. I loved the cool weather, the way the heat came up from vents in the floor, ballooning my dress, the red-gold leaves falling suddenly from the trees at each gust, and the delicate patterns of frost on the windows where I could spell out my name. I looked forward to Thanksgiving, not only because I'd be out of school for four days, but also because I'd have two big dinners that day with extra desserts. One at noon with our family—chocolate cake with fudge icing—and the second in the evening with the Flanagans, who always had homemade apple pie.

And yet Thanksgiving morning we woke to a shock: We would *not* be going to the Flanagans after all. Sixteen-year-old Mary Alice had eloped the night before with the silent, handsome Mitchell! My mother, talking on the phone to Mrs. Flanagan, was distraught, as if Mary Alice was her very own daughter. As she poured coffee for herself and my father, she said sadly, "Well, there goes Mary Alice's adult life!"

Somehow in the midst of the conversations that followed about Mary Alice, I assumed that she would have a baby. She didn't have a baby that year, but I remember the edge of concern over the possibility, something women talked about in lowered voices when my sister and I came into the room. Of course, we heard all the undertones, the worried phrases "She had such potential!" and "It's a tragedy" even in the hushed voices of the women who played bridge with my mother. And we knew that women often had babies once they were married. Mostly I felt mad at Mary Alice, who still wore pleated skirts and mohair sweaters and probably continued to tack up pictures of heroes on her vanity, because she'd disappointed me and would now have a life of closets and cellars, or some mundane equivalent. The arc of her life had suddenly gone flat.

When I went back to school after Thanksgiving, I met Peter in the cloakroom. He smiled at me and held out the candy he'd brought me wrapped up in aluminum foil with an orange ribbon on the top. I took the candy cautiously, not sure if this meant we were tied to each other, and if so exactly what that entailed. It was my earliest concern about relationships: that gifts often implied more than their surface pleasure. I worried suddenly that he might ask me to elope as his brother Mitchell had done with Mary Alice, and before we left the cloakroom, I turned to him and said peremptorily, "I'm not having any babies!" and walked briskly out into the room, relieved to have said my piece.

During elementary school, when my sister and I played dolls, we never let them have babies. Perhaps the stories of young girls in trouble, or girls like Mary Alice who would no longer go out into the world, had struck home, making us queasy about letting our young dolls become mothers. We loved grown-up Madame Alexander dolls instead of Betsy Wetsys and demanded that they do absurd but interesting things such as sing loud, smaltzy songs in nightclubs, have a house with the roof open to the stars, or best of all, live in Greenwich Village and work as a window designer at Bloomingdale's. Of course, we combed and washed our dolls' hair, dressed them for exotic dates, but our imaginations never took us into the heated interior of family life. Instead, we gave them dancing lessons, clarinet lessons, baton lessons, swimming lessons, mimicking the way we spent most of our time.

While I was in elementary and junior high school, my mother drove my sister and me forty miles back and forth four days a week on two-lane blacktop roads to lessons in distant cities. I'd sit in the backseat, one leg tucked under me, the other swinging idly as I stared at the flat, plowed fields the color of old stew meat. As we rode, I could feel the expectations humming from the dashboard of Mother's car, spinning out over the upholstered seat as we moved toward the four-way stop at County 102. Can you do the front walkover flip, your part of the pas de deux? Can you play the new Bach sonatina? The Mozart sonata? These lessons were to make us "cultured" so that when we moved to the city we would be like the sophisticated natives who understood that an evening spent at the Ballet Russe de Monte Carlo was an evening of pleasure and refinement. Of course, we'd wear fur coats and long dresses, have opera glasses and tiaras. We'd be glamorous as all get out. We'd be girls, but with all the independence of boys.

Growing up, my father always teased us, saying he'd wanted five boys and one girl. "Look what I got!" he'd say in mock despair while my sister and I buttered our toast and shot annoying glances at my brother. Though we girls became "honorary sons," these actual words were never spoken. Instead, the idea was intuited in the hallways of our imaginations, in the public life demanded by its applause. And it was applause we wanted, great rolling rounds of it, like putting a seashell to your ear and hearing only clapping. Standing ovations would be even better! The point of life, I decided, was figuring out just how to get your due. And in some sense how to turn girlhood into boyhood, into the kind of approval that shouted its good news.

Although my mother often lived both roles—having a career as a biology teacher and taking care of house and children—she never taught my sister and me any homemaking skills. "What's this?" I asked, holding up a sieved bowl. "A colander," she answered, taking it from me and draining the spaghetti. That was it. End of lesson. We never learned how to cook, sew, or clean house—"This is a dust mop," my mother-in-law said when I got married, "This is Windex"—and yet despite these absences in our education, our daily lives were intimately connected to the feminine. We knew, for instance, that the female world was divided into mothers and nonmothers and, like many children who easily hold a contradictory idea in their heads, we saw there was something eccentric, sad, even peculiar about the childless women who occasionally surrounded us. In my mind, these women were failures not because they didn't have children, but because they hadn't gotten out of town, hadn't done something fabulous.

We often heard hushed conversations in the kitchen between such women and our mother about some aspect of their "difficulty." Nobody mentioned the word infertility. That would be indelicate, impolite. I imagined my second grade teacher, Mrs. Perry, leaving school with our stack of spelling words and printing exercises, driving home to a lonely, dark house in Bon Secour where she spent three hours in solitude waiting for her husband to get home from work. Solitude seemed the enemy in a region defined by gregariousness. In my own yard playing on the jungle gym with my friends, I tried to imagine what Mrs. Perry would do with those idle hours. Maybe she soaked her feet in Epsom salts as Mother occasionally did when she'd had a long day, or perhaps she made curtains and bedspreads as Mrs. McTeague sometimes did when her kids were at the swimming pool. She certainly would be relieved of the many tasks of chauffeuring kids around to dentists and Cub Scouts. Sometimes while I climbed crablike across the bars, I imagined Mrs. Perry sitting slumped in a chair, her hands hanging limply down the sides, her face numb with the emptiness of her life. More than anything I wondered why she had not gone to live in New York, where there were crowds of people moving about at all hours, where she could go to the Museum of Natural History and be face to face with dinosaur skeletons or Eskimo dioramas. She could visit the famous public library.

It wasn't until late adolescence that I saw an escape from my conflict with achievement. It was so close at hand, it was almost a joke, a quick slide into hiding. Though I didn't feel female, how easy it was to mimic the world of the feminine: knees together, back straight, my mind a cloud of potential fashions. Spaghetti straps or strapless? Bikinis? Pedal pushers? Spike heels or square-toed flats? There was so much to assess—how to be that perfect object, sweatless, smooth, nipples never pointy, hair neatly brushed. And yet all the time I was secretly practicing for this pastel life, ambition throbbed deep inside my bones. My sister had been racking up awards, proving herself in the masculine/feminine territory we traversed. Not only was she awarded a National Merit Scholarship and several valedictory prizes, but she was also the Speckled Trout Rodeo Queen, with her picture in the paper, a crown on her head.

I paled by comparison—no awards, no publicity—but I didn't know the route out of envy. Instead I embedded myself in the female world, turning ambition to artifice, constructing beauty as my entrance into the world. Getting dressed for a school dance was nothing less than a theatrical production. I could have been a character in a play: the face, body, and style transformed from the ordinary to the exotic. First the face had to be contoured, the false eyelashes applied, the eyebrows drawn on, the cheeks sculpted. Then the hairpieces were fixed into place. Each night I rolled the fake bangs on an orange juice can so they would be slightly curled rather than poker straight, ready to be attached to my scalp with bobby pins. Then a headband obscured the bobby pins from the world. For certain dresses I wore a waist cinch that gave me my Scarlett O'Hara look, the stays splicing my ribs like punishing fingers, spiky and stiff. After my disguise was complete, I stared at myself in the mirror and whispered, "Hello," as if acquainting myself with a new creature. But I didn't really know what my transformation meant. I knew only that zeal was what counted, and now I was a dark object palpitating with fierceness.

I took my fierceness like a wrapped secret to college. At age nineteen, if there was any sleeping core of longing in me, it was a desire to feel female, to make the inside and outside cohere. *What would it mean to feel womanly?* I wondered. *Did other women feel this alienated from themselves?* I didn't know. I didn't even know how to ask. Instead, I kept my anxiety inside the locked box of my psyche and waited for what would happen next. What happened next was that I met a man I was crazy about, a man who became my boyfriend, a man who pulled me into the packed darkness of his closet, pressing me against his blue work shirts, soft from so many washings, and said, "I love you." Through the open closet door, Jimi Hendrix's "Purple Haze" drifted in, the guitars whining with sexual energy. I felt thrilled to the bone. My boyfriend's lips nuzzled at my ear, my hair, my neck. "I want you to have my babies," he whispered. I snuggled closer. For a single instant, the inside and the outside seemed to meet. "Yes," I said. "Yes."

Once I had a house and a husband, I wanted that world, the female world of lemon-pine odors and baking bread, of worry over curtain length and where to hang the oval mirror. And yet I stood in the kitchen and did not know what to do. It was a huge room, odd in its regularity, with too much linoleum and chrome, gadgets, and wood. I didn't know how to work the stove, the electric can opener, the double boiler, the meat thermometer. I had no idea what to cook, how to make a meal so that everything came together at the same time. Eventually Ray's parents sent over Loretta, their cook, to supervise my learning, to direct me in the meals of their family: chicken and dumplings, hot water cornbread, blackberry cobbler, creamed corn, stuffed tomatoes, hush puppies, sweet potato pie, and last but not least, stewed cabbage. It was the stewed cabbage that stumped me, those hard clumps of roughage turning too quickly to mush on the bright new eyes of the stove.

"Heat too high," Loretta would say when I passed the pot of limp cabbage to her for approval. She never looked at me when she spoke, but instead focused on an unassuming spot on my neck and locked her eyes into position.

"What?" I'd ask, trying to break her gaze, to make her acknowledge that I was there, standing right beside her.

But she pretended not to hear, so I tried again, cutting the cabbage into halves, then quarters, then eighths, slicing the fatback into thick awkward fingers of lard, adding just enough water to cover the top.

After two days I thought I had the hang of it. When Loretta was there, the cabbage came out tender, soft (not mushy), and tasted surprisingly sweet to my tongue. (Who could ever think of cabbage as lyrical, as sweet, soft curls that slide down your throat?) But on the days I tried preparing it alone—following her instructions meticulously—it came out soggy as wet bread or else hard and crunchy like raw potato. I spent at least five minutes each day throwing away ruined cabbage. After six months I gave up on domesticity, fixed hamburgers and pizza, and went back to college in Memphis. My past had risen up to claim me.

And yet the tapestry of my life remains a chaos of unraveled threads. I spent the entire marriage watching for a sign of who to become. Yet no sign appeared. No treasure fell from the sky. No trap door opened. After the marriage fell apart I realized that the waiting had been for nothing, that the one positive result of the marriage had been its infertility. I was grateful I wouldn't be a single mother, a child-mother, and settled down to live alone for six years, studying art, taking classes at the university, drawing designs and portraits alone in my room. I was happy in a rebellious sort of way, like a bird gaining its wings and flying directly into a whirlwind.

In my room I pared everything down to essentials: bed, chair, table, lamp, art supplies, camera. Here I felt monkish, transfixed, a potential honorary son. From this perspective, my past life looked like a lull in a storm, the dead center of a hurricane. Before I'd wanted a protective cloak, one that would diminish the effects of the outside world and keep me young and smooth like a wrapped chocolate inside a box. Now I wanted high winds. I immersed myself in art, working seven days a week, going to a Rothko exhibit or seeing works by Billy Al Bingston and Acconci, listening to Laurie Anderson and Philip Glass every weekend, trying to fashion a life. During this period I never thought about children, about anything that would divert me from my newly claimed world. I was in my late twenties, without a boyfriend. If anyone had asked me if I wanted children, I'd have shrugged and said,

"Who knows? There's still plenty of time to worry about that," and moved into the darkroom, setting up the enlarger, the trays of developer and fix, getting out my film from its plastic sheets.

And there was still time. Yet the imaginative life is a quirky life often tied to the unfinished business of childhood. For me that meant continually straddling the masculine/feminine domain, confronting my ineptitude in both spheres. Although I saw art—and then, later, writing—as my salvation, the thing that made me invisible, translucent, a mind and body exploding onto cloth and film and paper, it satisfied only one part of the equation. Ritualistically, the feminine demand for seduction still reared her insistent head, and there would be days when I had a love affair with the mirror or when I lay on the couch obsessed with a recent infatuation, like the one I had with Russell.

I met Russell in 1978 when he walked through the art department at UCLA, looking sleepy eyed and cynical. He stopped beside one of my art projects: two 1950 red Chevrolet doors with Expressionist portraits of me in the windows—a dark-shadowed girl with the depressive gaze of the Romantics. He smiled—the corners of his mouth barely turned up—then looked up at me and said, "You should come over."

Well, I came over. I looked at his work—took two paces back and commented on the subtlety of the gray lines, how they counterbalanced all the peeled-looking white space, the rubbed-out salmon edges—all the while reeling with desire. The next morning I stood around in his studio kitchen—a bare cupboard, a coffee pot, a toaster—in my underwear, waiting for the coffee to perk, for Russell to finish sealing a painting, for a reason to go home. I told myself this thing with Russell was nothing, a fling, but I seemed unable to do any work while my body breathed sex. Instead I bounced around his studio, straightening the bedspread, trying on different clothes, washing my hair, cutting off my jeans. It was as if art had never existed and I was once again a teenager, caught in a new and more sophisticated trap. Sex was like a giant rubber band, and I kept crawling around its loop, sniffing for clues, looking for a way to move faster, to stop. When would the sex connect with something deeper, more permanent? Did I want it to, or would I keep moving around this circle forever, never getting anything done?

One afternoon I walked alone in the astringent California light, squinting at the palms, at the hot-blooming hibiscus, and I sensed, as if it was a smell in the air, that I would not move further around the track with Russell. After three months I went diligently back to work, the affair ended, my brain refocused like a needle following its path inside a groove.

When I met David a year later at age thirty, I'd just finished my MFA in art. I was making collages of cloth, poems, and photographs, assembling these on a long table in the middle of my apartment. Almost immediately we began to argue, bickering like street children, shouting out our opinions about art—the typical battle of aesthetics, old code/old form vs. new code/new form and the legitimacy of all combinations in between—while sipping espresso at the boulangerie or driving on the freeway to Torrance or Long Beach to pick up supplies. With David I didn't stop working but simply moved my supplies across the room from his in the studio where we lived. It was a huge box of a room—all concrete with eight-foot ceilings, no windows, only double garage doors that swung out like wings into a dirty alley bordered by chain-link fences and signs that read: BEWARE ATTACK DOGS. If I stood in the doorway, I could smell Mexican cooking down the alley, the greasy mixture of onions and beans. We were five miles from Venice Beach, where the roller skaters had taken over the boardwalk and muscle builders pumped up while watching the roar of the ocean. We slept in a loft and cooked on a hot plate. With a refrigerator, a shower, workspace, and a darkroom, we considered our lives complete. We stayed up all night working, then slept until midafternoon. We thought of ourselves as bold and sacrificial, having nothing to do with bourgeois life. And yet the reality is we were simply poor.

We were part of an underclass culture barely able to sustain our current lifestyle, sometimes trading work for rent. Of course, we didn't have health insurance. We didn't even have car insurance.

By this time my sister had finished her medical degree, had gone into practice, had birthed her first child. "You'd better watch out," she told me conspiratorially over the phone, "the women in our family are exceptionally fertile. All I have to do is tell my husband I want to get pregnant, and the next month I am." I laughed with her over the phone, the very idea of me, *me,* getting pregnant. "I'm a long way from that!" I said, looking across the room at *The Raft of Medusa,* my latest art piece. I wished suddenly that she could see it, the layered collage of dyed cloth, the draped netting, torn and gaping, the reedy bamboo. It would surprise her, stem the tide of her accomplishments. From a distance her life looked like a perfect performance, one that happily combined the roles I was still trying to sort through. It seemed natural to me that her life should be jammed tight with obsession, with diversity, while I was still trying to master one straight line.

During the next three years, my sister often called and asked me when David and I were getting married, and more important, when we were going to have children. While she talked, I stared at the concrete slab floor, the raised scratchy surface we hosed down to clean up, the puddles of water drying near the door. The tables held splotches of dried paint. We hung our clothes on a clothesline that traversed one corner of the room, their spooky shadows shifting with each gust of wind. "Ground control to Major Tooommmm," floated out the window from a neighbor's stereo above the clink of dishes, the mumble of voices. My sister had no real sense of our situation, our poverty. And I'd never felt comfortable telling her that we'd chosen this, that we'd consciously given up making money in exchange for time to make art. Of course, we had jobs, but they were simply that, incidental ways to make rent money. Never careers. By this time my sister had had two more children, had brought a partner into her practice, had added a string of bedrooms onto her house. "My kids need some cousins," she said, pretending to tease, but I caught the serious note in her voice. "Surely, you don't want them to grow up without cousins!"

I assured her that I didn't, then went back inside the darkroom and switched on the enlarger. I knew what my sister was saying. *You can be everything.* Didn't she have three children, a full-time profession? Didn't she race from office to home to grocery store with all the impetuous haste of our childhood? This was the message of the late seventies, the women's movement in full swing, women no longer choosing between career and motherhood, but having both. It seemed miraculous, almost a demand.

Yet at night in my dreams, I was always running—in and out of doorways, through fields of weeds, alongside dirt roads, the dust kicking up in a cloud at my heels. Usually I was running in terror, trying to escape some menace, unseen but real, in pursuit of my body, my soul. I was running, I now think, for two reasons: running *away* from the expectations of my culture to become a super woman, with both career and children—a woman who accomplishes everything the culture demands—and running *toward* a potential future, toward a realm I could claim. In my dreams I gave the truthful answer to my sister, the answer Sula Peace gives herself in Toni Morrison's *Sula:* "I don't want to make somebody else. I want to make myself."

On some unconscious level I knew that my quest for autonomy was my only chance for survival. And I'm convinced—though others might argue the point—that children change the autonomy of a woman's life more than any other condition. From my early age it was clear to me that I needed to live outside the "hive," as Virginia Woolf called the extended family circle. For a person overwhelmed by a crowd of three, this is important knowledge. When I began writing, I couldn't separate solitude from creativity. I hauled a desk upstairs into the loft where I could be entirely alone. It was hot and stuffy. It smelled like musty sheets and dried apples. Spiders drifted down, each hanging suspended on one silken thread. I admired them. Like me, they worked alone. I needed this atmosphere of silence, of heat, of dust motes swimming in the light. Through writing, my body taught me that my choice of solitude was not selfish but necessary, a blossoming, a way of growing up to a self I could love.

This perspective came clear to me one day recently when I was lying in bed, listening to the early morning sounds of my neighborhood—the hiss of school bus brakes, the banging of car doors, the stutter of cold engines—and I felt for the first time the strength and diversity of my needs. For so long I had felt limited by them, ashamed. But this morning the decisions in my life were mine. Soon I would get out of bed and work on a novel. I could already feel the pen in my hand, see the cup of hot tea on the table. Solitude beckoned. . . . I would be alone but not lonely, distracted only by the ticker tape in my own head. I thought suddenly of my early imaginings of Mrs. Perry, about her lonely afternoons, her fearful wait for old age. I couldn't help but smile at these misperceptions. What if instead of her feet in Epsom salts, her mind slurred by emptiness, she was home dreaming a dream like I was: immersed in a manuscript, her mind making its own convoluted web, each word drawing her closer to that internal mystery that is the self unlocking slowly from its knot, like fingers from a fist.

A LETTER TO SOUTHERN GIRLS ABOUT BEAUTY

I know, I know, the last thing you want is to hear an older woman lecturing you about beauty. You've heard enough from my generation—the Women's Movement Generation—about inner beauty, self-worth, and the importance of taking yourself seriously instead of staring for hours in the mirror, agonizing about the length of your hair or the thickness of your thighs. You've probably had your fill of complaints about piercing and tattooing and wearing those see-through tops. But that's not what I want to say.

Okay, I'll tell it straight. Beauty matters. And yet what I'm struck by is that beauty isn't what most people think. Or not *only* what people think. It's not just hair and eyes and boobs and hips. It's not just how you look in an evening gown or a bikini. It's something more oblique, more private than that, something that rises up in the act of living, becomes luminous and vital and alive, embellishing whatever features and figure you have. Now, before you think that's a complete cop-out, let me explain.

I spent *years* in harness to the mirror, obsessed over every bit of myself—from my eyebrows down to my toenails—and then I wiggled out of that trap like an animal shedding its skin. I wiped off my makeup and let my hair run wild. During this period I went home one Christmas to a small Alabama town with its narrow dirt roads and blue sultry skies. It was sometime in the middle eighties, when the whole country saluted wealth and self-interest, when women were getting their boobs done and their hair foiled and my own sister, decked out in suede, was circling her arms with diamonds that sparkled in the sunshine and glittered like underwater prisms in their dark, secluded boxes.

Well, you can imagine that I stood out like a martian. My hair had grown long and uneven; my clothes were strictly T-shirts and jeans and a faded denim jacket with the pockets ripped out. I didn't wear eyeliner or powder; the most I could agree to was a smear of lipstick. Light coral.

What pulls me back to that Christmas visit is an afternoon when I was in the car with my sister. We were on our way to Pensacola, Florida, to buy another present for her daughter for Christmas. Probably a pretty sweater or a coat or some fashionable ankle boots. I can't remember what it might have been, but in the course of the trip my sister told me about a kind of cosmetic surgery she wanted to have, some knife trick to whisk away the tiny red veins that tangled beneath the skin of her nose. "They drive me crrrra-azy," she said, glancing quickly at me. "Absolutely nuts. Every time I look in the mirror, that's all I see. I'm *not* gonna have a Karl Malden nose."

I gave her an anxious, aggrieved look, as if she'd just told me she wanted to become a reptile.

"What?" she said, looking at me.

"That's absurd!" I stared past her to the blaze of Christmas decorations on the houses we passed, all reds and greens and shiny golds. "You've got all this energy, all these good things in your life, and you're worrying about *your nose?*" My disdain, I realize now, was almost palpable.

My sister tightened her grip on the steering wheel and stared straight ahead. "Yep, that's what I'm worrying about, and if you weren't so self-righteous about your own views, you'd see that it matters to me."

"Oh, I see that it matters to you," I said. "And that's what worries me. You're starting to be irrelevant."

We had come to a curve in the highway, and my sister almost ran off the road. She pulled over with a squeal of brakes, stopped the car, and turned around angrily. "What's *wrong* with you? What's gotten into your head? For God's sake, you're taking this feminism thing too far.

You think women don't worry about beauty anymore because you've decided not to worry about beauty. But for you, it's just the flip side of the same coin. One day you're obsessive; the next day you denounce whatever you used to be obsessive about. You're just as fucked up about the whole beauty thing as you ever were."

At that moment I thought about getting out of the car and walking home, but it was twenty miles of swampland and straggly pines, and though I wanted to be rebellious, to stick up for my side of things, I knew I'd never make those twenty miles. Instead, I looked out the window at a fir tree circled in red blinking lights. That single glance gave her an advantage.

"God, you're such an idiot," she said.

"Well, at least I'm not a traitor."

"At least *I* don't pretend to be what I'm not."

"Sure, but you've got your priorities all screwed up."

"Says Miss Know-It-All who still can't stand to have an ounce of fat around her waistline."

She had me there. I felt a secret pride in my thinness, my swivel hips, my svelte body. If I ever gained weight, I'd be the first person to go on a crash diet, even though I didn't believe in such diets, thought them harmful, destructive. I'd be eating spinach or sucking up some awful diet product and jumping on the scales every thirty minutes to see if anything had changed. But I didn't want to admit it. What I wanted to say was that I'd given up beauty, or at least the earnest pursuit of beauty, in an effort to have a voice, to learn to speak in the world without deflection or deceit. And yet as my sister and I yelled at each other, I couldn't help but wonder if beauty and respect had to be so mutually exclusive—voice/body—like two sides of a coin. Heads or tails.

After our skirmish we sat in huffy silence, me sagged against the door, my sister slumped against the seat. It was then that she laughed. A furtive, I-don't-give-a-damn kind of laugh. "You remember we both wanted to be Miss America." She fingered her nose. "Well, for-get that!"

"Speak for yourself," I said, but I couldn't help smiling, remem-bering how we used to wrap ourselves in towels and parade through the bedroom, blowing kisses to the crowd.

Just thinking about this shared past, something loosened in me, and as we drove toward Pensacola, I knew that some of what my sister said was true. Why, even denying beauty took a certain amount of energy each day; I had to will myself *not* to look in the mirror. Worse, I had to consciously stop the buzz in my head, the constant assessment of each woman I saw: *funky haircut; too much eye shadow; uh, oh, getting a chicken neck.* I did this kind of tallying unconsciously, systematically, as if I was a casting director for a soap opera. Such criticism, I hoped, was only the residue of my cultural training. *Enough,* I told myself.

Still, days came when I wondered if I'd simply mistaken an inner thought, *the desire to be taken seriously,* for an outer correlative, *the body stripped of cosmetic embellishment,* as if a plain exterior suggested an intel-lectual interior, as if outer purity proved inner worth. The truth is, that's exactly what I believed. More than anything, I wanted to strip myself down to the expression of my thoughts. I wanted to get rid of the body, to be all thought, all essence, all knowing. That's what men did, I believed, and during this phase, it seemed the only answer to respect.

But the body is a powerful thing, a demanding thing, and about six months after that trip to Pensacola, I opened my eyes one day and knew that I hadn't let go of my desire for beauty. I got up and looked in the mirror, wanting once again to put on a little mascara, to have my hair lightened. Was that a new wrinkle around my mouth? A gray hair in my eyebrows? I gave myself the once-over from several different angles before despair took over and I fled outside. You might say that, once again, I chose beauty. Not the serene classical beauty of fine fea-tures and a chiseled profile. Not the commercially sexualized beauty so popular on TV and in the ads I see in magazines. Nothing like that. This time, it had to be something more.

What I remember is this: After I looked in the mirror, I walked to the end of a rickety pier at Soldier Creek, where a mist rose from the water, shadowing the bamboo near the water's edge and clouding the banks full of willows and weeds. A heron began its slow, awkward flight. I watched as it settled on a grassy island, standing in absolute stillness, one leg raised. Nothing moved except the occasional ripple of a fish beneath the water, prodding the skin of the creek. And yet everything inside me was manifested in this landscape, this moment, this physical radiance. My body lightened. My spirit lifted. I felt ridiculously alive, as if I could do anything in the world without embarrassment or self-consciousness, as if every thought had legitimacy and vitality. My body, my face, was no longer a hindrance, a disgrace, but simply the physical manifestation of my being. How had I missed this before? Why had I been so blind? The truth is I'd known it and buried it and then forgotten that I knew it. That was the puzzle. The world, so full of beauty, was to be shared, absorbed into the body . . . and given back. Beauty, I suddenly understood, had not so much to do with makeup or hairstyles or fashionable clothes, but with the grabbing hold of your own erotic energy and putting it to use. Lipstick or no lipstick was beside the question. What was essential was passionate attention, a leaping beyond the self.

"That's silly," I hear you say. "That's just intellectual hype. Pretty girls get all the good things and you know it."

Well, they did in my day too. But my quibble is with that word "all." Pretty girls don't get all the good things. They get attention and popularity, and that's why we envy them. They get "immediate" attention, the head-turning kind. Call it instant power. Protection. Freedom from scorn. And yet something lies beneath this, something that no one wants to talk about. It's what beauty engenders.

You probably think I'm talking off the top of my head, so let me speak from experience. For one year, a long time ago, I had beauty, and the knowledge of it changed everything. No longer did I feel I had no resources to demand attention, enter conversations, and secure favors. Everything positive I'd heard and read about beauty seemed electrified, a caveat that had fallen into my lap through no effort of my own. I'd simply let my hair grow out to spread in a curly mane around my shoulders and taken the wraps off a lanky, slender form, dressing in sundresses and sandals and allowing the sun to freckle my shoulders as I walked through town. Perhaps this confession smacks of foolish pride. Even nostalgia. But keep in mind, *it was only one year*. Even now I wonder why beauty had to be such a laconic gesture. So fickle, such a short, wistful bloom. And yet, if I'm honest, I'm glad I had my one year, glad I learned both the power and the constraints of beauty, glad that I began to see how I might have lived if that beauty had continued. Surely I'd have been its slave, seduced into being the seducer, seeking always the redemptive moment when beauty would do its work, make others compliant, curious, and give me an instant reading of sexual relationship.

Why do I say that?

Because what that year taught me, and still teaches me, is that those who are beautiful are encouraged by our culture to believe implicitly in the conversion experience, to believe that their beauty is the catalyst for salvation, the means to an end. Our society smothers us with this tricky myth: If you are beautiful, it says, your life should be redeemed, gratified, transformed. The wheel of fortune should stop its frantic turning. I remember a late spring evening during "my year" when, dressed in a dark-green knit dress that hugged my body and accentuated my blonde hair and fair skin, I was to meet a famous novelist who had just moved to our town. In my mind, this dress was my introduction, a red flag of attention that said, *Look at me! Admire me!*

The famous novelist was in his early forties, thin and awkwardly dressed, but with a shy ease that made me hope for the best. After I was introduced to him, we talked comfortably for a few minutes about the town and the community of writers. Then after this brief conversation, my husband asked the man a question about politics, and they began a heated discussion about Clinton. The man's face brightened. He ran his fingers through his hair. Their shoulders moved imperceptibly closer as the talk deepened. I was furious. Wasn't I the writer? Hadn't I worn the pretty green dress? Could I be so easily deflected, drummed out of the conversation? I had no investment in Clinton, nothing pertinent to say.

And yet, none of these things mattered. The green dress didn't matter. The topic of conversation didn't matter. Being a writer didn't matter. What mattered was that I had hoped to influence a man by my presence, to entice and seduce, regardless that the seduction would be only vicariously sexual. I had made the classic female mistake, assumed that beauty was more important than ideas. But beauty is never more important than ideas except in the arena of sexual seduction. Even then, it's no guarantee. But old habits die hard. I had grown up with the belief that my presence mattered, that my influence was physical and sexual, although I'd coated that thought with a patina of sophistication. I could talk books and literary criticism, but as I put the green dress in the very back of the closet—never to be worn again— I realized that ideas were still the cover story for me, beauty the plot. My sister had been right. I had not grown savvy about beauty, had not put that baby to bed.

Am I smarter now? Yes. If nothing else, age will demand a new perspective, make you sit up and take notice of other things. At age fifty-three I went on a book tour, and what I remember is a particular talk that I gave. It wasn't in a big city or at a big college but at a junior college in a working-class town where many of the people in the audience were retired high school teachers and factory workers. I had my misgivings. I hadn't felt well that morning and had no sense of the audience until I walked into the room. I don't remember what I looked like, have no idea what I wore. What I remember is the feeling of inti-

Goody-Goody Girls ────────────

The building rose dark and mysterious at the edge of a small Alabama town. There was something odd about it, not the red brick masonry or the shaggy mass of scrubs clustered around its perimeter, but the listless sigh of silence as if the building had long been napping. *Creepy,* I thought as I followed the other student nurses my mother was chaperoning into the broken strangeness of the state mental hospital. I remember the dimness of the entryway, the ill-lit stairs as we wound our way up to the wards, my sister and I, aged ten and nine, walking singly but holding hands, openly wary of thick, ugly walls and anorexic light slicing through the windows, a pale, gloomy thread. Though it was the end of the fifties, we could have been winding our way up a seventeenth-century tower where political prisoners were held, where foul deeds had been hastily done. Just when I thought I couldn't breathe this sharp, antiseptic air another minute, the head nurse thrust open the door to a large, bright room where glorious light poured through the windows, haloing the patients who sat slumped like sacks in their chairs, their mouths running with a juice that was more than plain drool. They were mostly old women gone to fat, or rail thin, their heads sunk into shoulders, feet entwined around the legs of a chair. I stood close to my mother, afraid that someone might jump out of a closet, might gouge out my eye with a spoon. Instead, a natty old woman, toothless, her thin gray hair covering the patchy baldness of her head, pointed at us. "Good girls," she screeched, her eyes gleeful, manic. "Goody-goody girls!"

The other patients remained silent, inscrutable, as lost in unreachable lives as Beckett's Mr. Endon in the Magdelena Mental Mercyseat. Most of the patients looked stunned, sitting and staring, playing their fingers against their knees, rubbing their breasts or their stomachs as if searching for erotic arousal. I stared at them intensely, covertly, from behind lidded eyes, certain that only failure and shame could turn you into such a mess.

It was failure I was most afraid of, but shame caught at my heels, bumping behind me like a tin can attached by a string to my foot. Both fears came to me prematurely, fatally, and by the time I was in Miss Williams's fourth grade class, I worried obsessively about my public fate, longing only for protective coloring. As I walked to the pencil sharpener, I shivered at the thought of being tortured like Glenda Hennessy, so hugely fat the boys called her "The Explosion" and made farting sounds when she lumbered by. They tripped her, taunted her, threw spitballs at the fleshy spill of her knees. More than anything I wanted to be normal, accepted, to collect all the tokens of privilege: compliments, praise, encouragement, desire. Who cared what it cost? What mattered the lies, the betrayals, the silence? Dogged by fear, I thought my problem must surely be my hair, the way it fuzzed out in a frizzy halo like Little Orphan Annie's, or sometimes on rainy days kinked up like Buckwheat's. I'd be walking home from school, caught in a delicious dream about how I'd grow up and marry my teacher, Miss Williams, the two of us living in a white cottage by the sea with seashells on every windowsill and a teapot on the table decorated with English ivy, when Tommy Bodenheimer or Jimmy Sales would whiz by on their bikes, yelling "Frizzball! Frizzball!" then clutching themselves as if they were having heart attacks. They laughed delightedly while anger sneaked up my chest, swelling in the tightness of my throat. I took off after them, hell bent to leather, until I saw Mrs. Bodenheimer turn from hanging wet sheets on the line and fix me with a withering glare. Suddenly I froze, shame covering my rage like a glove, protecting it so that no one could imagine it was there. I touched my hair, then waved timidly at Mrs. Bodenheimer until she nodded and went back to untangling her sheets.

Rage, I learned early, was unacceptable—"Girls, control your tempers!" Mrs. Ellison yelled to us daily as we squabbled over paper dolls and fierce games of jacks. "There's no need for a hissy fit."

"If you raise your voice one more time," Miss Bloom, the crafts teacher at Sunday school, said when we burst out in fury over a decoupage project, "you will be *permanently* excused." There seemed no way around it: Women in our small Alabama town had to be good. And "good" meant silent. It was a law.

Oh, occasionally I'd see a woman in town slap a child, hissing "Stop-pit!" in a tight, hushed voice when her boy grabbed at Halloween masks or tried to eat three pieces of caramels at one time. Then the mother would look up in embarrassment, smile feebly, and brush the kid's hair out of his eyes, the world settling back to a comfortable rhythm of everyday niceness. As I watched these slight moments of distemper, my own worry increased, because what I felt was a dip into more dangerous waters, an anger that might send me screaming down the street, slapping at air. I knew I had to be careful, mindful not just of my manners, but of my very thoughts. Thoughts, I believed, could drive me into an avalanche of disasters, could wreck the fragile construction of normalcy I'd erected. I couldn't afford to fall apart, to be booby-trapped by my own furrowed mind. And so for years I watched from the sidelines while others "went off," cruising beyond the boundaries of normalcy, tempting fate, revealing themselves.

"Well, she just went off," a neighbor said to my mother about the girl in my ninth grade class who, for no apparent reason, quit going to school. And there was such a girl, a sweet, shy girl named Bonnie, smart in history and science, her thick mop of russet hair the kind I secretly envied, imagining myself with a mane of it flowing down my back, blowing out like a curtain in the wind. That hair seemed wasted on Bonnie, who kept it cut short, close to her scalp, leaving only the flap of bangs to hint at its beauty. I wondered if Bonnie ever thought about her hair as she dressed in oversized plaid dresses and tennis shoes and a tan car coat with fading red trim. She was quiet, intense, the kind of girl shadowed in the background, knowing the answer in American history and biology but seldom volunteering, staring instead at the scruff of clouds out the window while the correct answer was written right there on her page. I know because I often sat across from her. You could pass her in the hall and she'd look quickly down at the concrete as if memorizing the patterns of dirt and grime or at something in the distance that didn't really exist. I don't remember noticing her very much, though she was in several of my classes and sat beside me, her rather large feet taking up extra space in the aisle. She seemed frozen in silence, a scratch in the paleness of our class. And yet one day that silence began to change, hurtling from shyness into paranoia, so that she became afraid of everyone in the whole damn world. Or so our neighbor reported. "Went slap-dab crazy," she nodded, tapping her foot. "Loony."

But, of course, I have no idea what *really* happened.

What I do know is that I came home from school one afternoon, passed Bonnie's street, which wasn't far from my own. I was worrying about Mr. McFadden's final exam in history, about what kind of hair spray I'd buy—White Rain or Raynet—and which dress I'd wear to Ivy's party on Saturday night while Bonnie, in her room, had reached some sort of dead end. The very next day she refused to go to school, then refused the day after, then the day after that, though only three weeks remained in the term. *"She won't leave her house."* We heard it first as a rumor, gossip in the halls among the banging of lockers, the shrieking of freshmen, and we knew she'd taken a left turn to a place the rest of us were afraid to go. She'd "gone off," and no one could reach her now.

To my surprise she made one thing perfectly clear: She would see *no one*, would rush into her bedroom if Mrs. Spivey from across the street brought her mother a spinach casserole or if the postman came with a special delivery for her father. Even the principal, who was quiet himself, studious and restrained, with bifocals and a bushy gray

crew cut, had no luck with her. She turned stonily away from him, re-
fusing to come back to school, to finish the term.

I remember walking down her street on a hot summer day after the
school year was over, after I'd aced the history test, one I knew that
Bonnie would have aced too. As I edged nearer and nearer to her
house, I noticed it as if for the first time: a plain house, rectangular like
a box, but softened by shrubs, by the petunias and daisies her mother
had planted in the flowerbed near the steps. Irises bloomed in an innocent cluster beside the chain-link fence. *Bonnie lives in that house,* I
said to myself. I'd never really thought about this street, about the
pine straw that dusted the sides of the road, about the houses all neatly
arranged side by side, some with clotheslines in the backyards that you
could see from the street. Bonnie had seen this view every day as she
walked to school, probably had looked up at the branches of the
skinny pines, seeing snatches of blue and wishing that she inhabited
another life, any life. Mars couldn't be this terrible even if there wasn't
enough oxygen to breathe. Venus was surely a lovely planet, a place of
gossamer beauty, a veil of scent that kept you happy and high.

I wanted to step on the grass in her yard and peer into her room. I
imagined scratching my fingers on the mesh, calling out to her, my
girlish voice having just the right note of sympathy and respect. I
thought that somehow she'd meet me at her door, that I'd know exactly what to do. She'd ask me inside and for the first time we'd talk
the way people in books always talked, saying things with such clarity
and perception the mystery of life began to unravel, the two of us sitting side by side on her bed, conscientious, repressed, but lifting ourselves from the iron grip of sadness. In my mind, Bonnie told me what
was wrong, told me she'd been trying so hard—too hard—to be
good. And I knew she'd see that what was wrong with her was wrong
with me too. Wrong because we were both so terribly afraid, the fear
like a stalking beast that choked all the beauty from our thoughts. If
only I could talk to her I thought we might both admit that being

good was a dodge, a pretense, an escape, even though we had no other behavior to follow, no map of intriguing clues. As I strolled slowly toward her house, I thought of the afternoons I lay on my bed while *"nothing, nothing, nothing"* played its loop inside my head. It was like watching a ceiling fan in slow motion, the blades turning lethargically, barely moving though each infinitesimal motion was hypnotic, *nothing, nothing, nothing.* I was clearly depressed, but also incapable of articulating my sadness's depth or pitch.

Sometimes I'd catch my mother watching me, studying me when she thought I wasn't looking, and I knew what to expect, how the question would come, piggybacking on something innocuous about school, about a particular class, "How was that algebra exam yesterday?" she'd begin in a breathless voice as if there was a charge in the air, and then the inevitable, "Is everything *okay?*" said a bit too casually as she stirred her iced tea.

The only honest answer was No, but *that* would require an explanation, so I shrugged and said, "Sure," for fear is inexplicable, opaque, an impossible thing to explain. Fear is something good girls can't articulate. It's too vague, like smeared leftovers wrapped in layers and layers of plastic wrap. *What* is *that?* you think. Even unwrapped it looks suspicious, untidy. At fifteen I couldn't say exactly *what* I was afraid of except the unmentionable fear of failing so badly there would be nothing but a million pieces of me to pick up. Secretly I believed that inside me there was some kind of black goo, some mashed pulp like the sticky seeds of a papaya, and in dreams I saw my body exploding, the mess smearing, spreading, everybody stepping in it, then rubbing it disgustedly off of their shoes. The truth is I was afraid of ending up like Bonnie, my mind leaving a trail of garbage in its wake. So I courted caution like a mountain climber on a steep path, trained never to look down. And the amazing thing is that I didn't go off like Bonnie. Something kept me on course, going every day to school, to music lessons, to parties, to the National Honor Society Banquet at the end of the year, my hair teased in a bubble and sprayed with White

Rain. I graduated with honors: *The Girl Most Likely to Succeed.* A goody-goody girl.

I never did sneak up to Bonnie's window. I never talked to her and she never came back to school, though something had caused her to stay in her room, hiding, just as I was hiding, except there was, I believed, this difference: Bonnie had removed all the masks. I imagined that she stood in the white light of all that fear, finally revealing it to herself, and the very exposure shut her down. Secretly I admired her for it, and yet knowing such defeats were possible, I became extra careful not to look too closely at what was going on inside my head. Instead, that summer I read books that might get me into college, played tennis, and took swimming lessons, perfecting my backstroke.

Only at the end of summer did I walk again past Bonnie's house, moving into the cooler shade of the oak trees that formed a canopy where the street intersected with Main. Here the houses were older, bigger, not elegant but with screened-in porches where women sat and smoked Vantage cigarettes, their hair teased weekly at Zade's Beauty Shop, their flowered house dresses ordered from Sears. They stared at whoever passed by, smoke streaming blue through the mesh, out into the still, hot afternoon air. "Hey, sweetie," they called and waved. I waved back. "Hey, Mrs. Anderson. Hey, Mrs. Paducah," then hurried on to the drugstore and stood at the magazine rack, paging through *Glamour* and *Vogue,* wondering how I'd ever get my hair to look tousled, my lips pouty, how I'd find the perfect diversion for safety.

Years go by and I skip ahead to my twenties, to graduate school in Los Angeles in the 1970s, where life is a different kind of hustle. Nestled inside me is the old cloak of goodness, but grafted to it like a starched inner lining, stiff and crackly, is the newness of intellectual hunger. Now goodness expands, swells, includes being smart, ironic, racing to the finish line with no visible damage. During my first fall semester I enroll in a seminar with a famous female artist who's rumored to be a "certified" genius, the darling of grant committees and galleries, the talk of the department. "She's so smart," Janice says when I tell her I'm taking Professor Norton's course, "she flat-out scares me." Even seated at her desk, Professor Norton looks intellectual with her thin, willowy frame, her darting gray eyes behind horn-rimmed glasses. She's pale, wan looking, as if, resistant to California, she shuns the sun, her eyes red rimmed like someone who reads late into the night.

Nervous about her class, I sit those first weeks in the small seminar room with the eucalyptus trees shading one side of the building, the stink of fear leaking from my underarms, a smell of burned coffee sweeping in from the lounge. Professor Norton sits before us and talks quietly—all of us straining forward—about the political concept of "otherness as a component of universality" while staring out at an empty California sky. When she stops midsentence, we hold our breaths, our minds crackling with expectation until she holds up one finger and slips out of the room to smoke a cigarette.

One day as she reads to us, she lifts her face from the book and stares into space as if she sees something the rest of us don't see. The light is dim in the room, the eucalyptus leaves pressed close against the window. She looks charged with anger and purity as she talks about contemporary art, as she mouths the words "conceptual art" with a bare hiss of breath. "My work is *conceptual*," she says, and I know the world is changed, the old one buried, lost, irrelevant. Gone is the sensuous, the intuitive, the poetic, while on the horizon lies the cerebral, the ironic, the political—always bold and unkind. And Professor Norton—looking into that anxious nothingness—has been chosen as the world's new goddess. I see this instantly, but I don't know what it can possibly mean.

I say very little in class, though each hour feels like a pressure cooker, my mind squeezed tighter and tighter into itself. It hurts to think. I'm not sure I can think. Each day I go home from class and lie on the floor in a kind of trance, a wet cloth on my forehead, waiting for the relief of darkness. Sometimes I sleep for hours then wake and begin the reading for the next week. Other times I distract myself with movies and cheap mystery novels. The class has no tests—making it difficult to judge my goodness—only a small paper and, of course, the discussion. Late at night I worry how she'll grade me, what criteria she'll use to define what I've learned, the extent of my "progress." I write down many ideas in that class, and yet even as I write I feel myself stiffen, harden as if a soft material inside me is solidifying. I take this for learning.

The morning my grades arrive, I anxiously rip open the envelope and stare in disbelief at the grade. Impossible! Ridiculous! I drop the paper to my bed and flee outside into the restless sun. She's a maniac, a crackpot. For hours I walk by the ocean, filling myself up with its fresh, clean breeze, picking up shells to put in my pockets, kicking sand, releasing all my nervousness and obsession. Then, in a fit of unusual clarity, I go back to my apartment and tear up the letter that says I've earned an A+ in Professor Norton's class.

It isn't until fall semester that I see her again. I'm hurrying into the elevator, hoping it will stay open so I won't have to take the stairs. I lunge into it, careening into its center a second before the giant doors whoosh shut. I have to catch my breath. I close my eyes, gasping. When I open them again, I realize I'm not alone, that a woman stands by the control panel, hunched toward it, coughing out a mad, demonic laugh. Her pale, thin arms are clenched against her chest, and she smirks at the floor as if enjoying the private leer of a dirty joke. It takes me a minute to recognize Professor Norton. Her hair's cut short in a kind of girlish bowl, her body in its print dress looks wasted, elbows pointy, knees knobby, her waist a flickering shadow. She doesn't look at me but mumbles to herself, her body wrapped in a tension all its own. I go with her past my floor, and when she gets off, I descend, standing in the hallway, looking out the big windows at the immaculate green grass, the landscaped yard, the trees that seem never to lose their leaves. For the first time I recognize this as an unnatural place.

Goody-Goody Girls | 69

"She's gone loony tunes," Janice says to me as she mixes indigo dye in small plastic bowls.

I squeegee the paint from my silk screen frame. "I wonder what happened. I wonder what made her go off." I want to know. I need to know. I understand those clenched, folded arms, that bent neck, the flurry of secrets that might spill into the air.

"No one knows," Janice says. "It could be *anything*."

Could it? I wonder. I can't quiet the thought that Professor Norton allowed herself to think too much about all the wrong things, but even as I ponder this I'm not sure what I mean. What ARE the wrong things? And yet as I clean up my dyes and paints, put away drop cloths and fabric, I realize with the certainty of a vision that my A+ wasn't unique. She gave one to each of us.

It was late afternoon when we left the mental hospital, the student nurses, my mother, my sister and me. After we'd looked at the crazies and they'd looked at us, we were escorted down that lonesome staircase into the frazzled heat of an April day, the sky just beginning to turn pink. The visit had made us all tired and we walked stooped, silent, the only sound the staccato click of Mother's high heels against the pavement. I know now that the student nurses were probably as nervous and tense as I was seeing people in that twilight of fear. Like me, they seemed glad to be outside, back in the world where dogs barked, women walked by with ordinary shopping bags in their arms, and the sun was slowly slipping behind the maples and pines. A crossing guard led a troop of Brownies across the street. Beyond us the cars waited at the far end of the parking lot; we knew the backseats would feel sticky with heat, the air like an oven, but for once no one would complain. As we moved toward them, one of the students turned to look at the windows of the day room where we'd visited. She stopped for a minute and just stared at them. "I bet they have a lot of secrets," she said, shaking her head, narrowing her eyes as if she could see those secrets hanging like bats over the patients, a thick black cloud. She looked so serious, but her words seemed hysterically funny to the rest of us. We laughed out loud, opening the doors to our cars, a shiver of relief flooding through us. If we could laugh, we knew we were all right, on the other side. Not yet knotted up by secrets.

But I was never sure. Both with Bonnie and the professor, only a thin veil separated them from me, a veil always in danger of tearing, splitting, ripping apart like rotten cloth, revealing a psyche with no shelter, no home, the secrets sharp as pointed sticks.

Secrets. Goody-goody girls. That was my secret.

For me goodness had nothing to do with saintly virtue, was no moral code that sprouted from my center. No, goodness was a tool, something I used as protection from the world of power, the world that was messy and dark and irrationally violent. Like many girls, I learned to defer, to apologize, to say what was expected in words that tiptoed into a conversation, barely touching their heels to the floor. Slyly, carefully, I hid what I felt to be true, imagining the heavy foot of authority stamping on the soft neck of my most intimate thoughts. The result, of course, was that a disguise took over, settling on my shoulders, tucking itself into my shoes, circling my waist. In time I no longer knew what I felt, no longer kept company with my own sentient world, that place where shadows bloom into thought and thought expands into vision. Instead, I became careful, walking around my small Alabama town as if I was generic, just any girl, the girl in the grocery store, the girl at the swimming pool, the girl sitting up in the bleachers devouring a Moon Pie. I liked to think of myself as offending no one. But, of course, by offending no one, I became nothing, and eventually the nothingness cut off my air. It took me years to figure out this simple thing: Fake goodness begets only violence to the self. And then there was this: a desertion. A divorce. A stranglehold of loneliness.

Of course, I never really knew if either Bonnie or Professor Norton was seduced by goodness. I only remember them both as quiet, intelligent people who seemed troubled, undone by the world. And yet

I was excited by their undoing, riveted by the mess they were making, waiting to see what would happen next. I watched their downward spiral with great fascination, buoyed by their despair, feeling each time I saw them, *there but for the grace of God, go I.*

And then, good girl that I was, I went there too.

INSIDE THE WRITING ROOM

I'm sitting on my front porch, looking at an essay I've just written. It made sense when I was formulating it in my head—cooking it, so to speak—but here on the page it's confusing, dull. I change a few verbs, rescue a sentence fragment, then trash the piece and walk downtown to buy a cup of coffee.

While I'm drinking my coffee, a friend comes by and asks what I'm doing.

"Brooding," I say. I tell her about the botched piece of writing and how the incarnation was so perfect inside my head.

"You've just forgotten," she says.

"What? What have I forgotten?"

"That writing is hard. You don't just get it down and earn your sigh of relief. You have to coach it and pamper it and baby it and rough it up a bit. You have to get your hands dirty. It's like doing two heart surgeries before lunch."

I laugh. I feel better.

I never thought I'd be a writer. I wasn't one of those kids who wrote poems and stories, who buried herself in books at age ten. Instead, writing took me by surprise. I began only after taking a course in Women's Autobiography while I was a student in art at UCLA. I was lucky enough to find a teacher who invited me to sit on her sunny porch to talk about writing. She looked at the poems I'd written and offered comments and suggestions. I went back to the studio where I lived, revised the poems, then burned parts of them for an art collage.

And then something happened. One day I lay down on my bed and read As I Lay Dying, *William Faulkner's book about the Bundren family. When I finished the book, I went into my study and wrote a story. Then I wrote another one. And another. It took me years to learn to write good stories and essays, but I've never regretted a minute. Writing forced me to look at the myths that crept along beside me, to see the characters who roamed around my perimeter and sneaked in close, pressing just beneath my skin. Writing forced me to shake the clutter out of my head and find something real and red hot, something burning. Everything that had bothered me rose to the surface, and I felt the singe of heat down my nerves.*

In many ways writing taught me how to think.

And that's what I want to do here: think about autobiography as both a genre and a process, think about writing as an act of faith as well as a road to self-discovery.

If only the past would let go and leave me in peace, I swear I'd be happy, serene. Yet even as I think this, the woodpecker outside my window begins his surgical clacking, a spider crawls up the slick bathroom wall, and I know there is no escape, that the nature of knowledge is tied to the nature of life.

So begins the tale of the autobiographer, a trapeze artist skimming lightly through air without a fictional net. Is this sheer vanity? Defection? A slap in the face of fantasy? Or is this a hint at the unwillingness of modern readers to surrender to disbelief?

Why *does* a modern writer attempt to knit up those bits of reflection we so grudgingly call "a life"? I could tell you that this is a revolutionary time in literary history. I could tell you that, in the words of Jill Ker Conway, "our culture dictates an inner script by which we live our lives," and our literary tribe is merely responding to this script. I could tell you that fiction has become cramped, too stingy and self-conscious to satisfy our greedy taste for revelation. But what any autobiographer secretly desires to tell is *how it began for me.* So let me open the floodgates of my writing life and allow the waters of memory to flow rudely through. Let me tell you a tale, not just the story of a genre but the story of a mind, what I've come to call My Savage Mind.

───────────

Like an old-fashioned story, I want to begin at the beginning, to immerse you in a time when I lived a bizarre, isolated existence in that most psychotic of cities, Los Angeles. It's here that fantasies are created, here that stretch limousines glide sleekly through traffic like worms tunneling through dirt, here that skaters race impetuously down the boardwalk, the fringe of their bikinis fluttering in the soft ocean breeze, here that homeless men sleep under my car, their legs, like fragile stalks, extending between the back tires. And it's here that I want you to see me: a young woman in her late twenties rushing down a busy freeway to a temporary word-processing job in midtown L.A. As in previous jobs I will become acquainted with no one, speak only the inevitable clichés, eat alone in the break room, then put a sign on my back that says *Typing for the Masses*. It's a stifling, numbing experience, and yet I do this for days, weeks, sometimes months without a bump in the routine, every cell in my body crying out for release, until the temp agency intervenes and I slink away to another dreary assignment. But that's only a part of me. The person you don't see in the office sits at her typewriter in the evening, poised as if at the crest of discovery, writing stories on paper squirreled away from her day job.

At night the ocean breeze whips at the filmy curtains, and smells of sulfur and jasmine float through the open doors, spreading their silky perfumes. I sit in my combination living room/kitchen and listen to the roar of the Pacific Ocean, to waves exploding against the shore, then retreating as suddenly as the release of a hand. Many days it is the only sound I want to hear, my mind tied to its erotic rhythm, its urgent exhalation. During this period my world is filled with clean-cut dichotomies: a day life of drudgery and boredom, a night life of tentative faith; a day life that is corporate and generic, a night life lifted by the voluptuousness of the sea. Sometimes when I'm stuck in a story, unable to create the next scene in my character's life, I walk out onto the roof and stare at the ocean as it rushes restlessly toward the shore, then retreats as if sucked back by an enormous, thirsty mouth. Outside, the sky is a calligraphy of stars, the night as pitch dark as the inside of my closet. On such nights I feel the curve of the universe, the promise of hope. But if I stay there long enough, I inevitably reflect on the fact that *this*—this life—is not where I was meant to end up: barely getting by, without full employment, no savings account or mortgage, much less health insurance or marriage. The truth is, I was groomed for success, meant to be a winner with college and graduate school, tutors and trainers, honors and awards. Clearly, I got up off the table before the operation was complete. Some mysterious angst made me throw away the mantle of improvement and slink quietly out of the room, content for a while to be a foot soldier, a subordinate, while I learned my nighttime craft.

And yet this failure was neither benign nor planned, a choreographed dance of stylized movement. It was more akin to the sudden flapping explosion of birds leaving a tree, bearing twigs and leaves and debris in their mouths. I left one world—the world of achievement—but carried its roiling imprint of success securely in my mouth.

I left because I'd discovered stories.

At night I bend over my desk, as immersed as an underwater swimmer who glides faithfully through black waters without the need for breath. I believe, perhaps naively, that writing fiction can illuminate the darkness, can split open the human boundaries that have narrowed to a tight slit. Each night I sit at my typewriter, listening to the buzz inside my head, seeing one character put a hat of trembling violets on her head while another kisses the inside of her palm, trying to get the kissing right. *Is this it? Mouth pinched, slightly puckered . . . no, no, mouth open, softly blooming.* Here is Dade staring at the desert, a wistful smile softening his sad, pockmarked face while tumbleweeds scatter just beyond him in the hot, glittery wind. Here is the Doctor's Wife haloing in and out of my vision, a specter of desire as she twirls and twirls, her arms spread out, her nightgown dipping and rising as she moves beneath the weeping willow tree.

Though I delight in these characters, an essential part of me remains baffled and detached as if my love for them can push down only so far before it hits a barrier, a grate, something hard slammed tight against my imagination. But what is that barrier, that grate?

In my stories I write exclusively about the American South, pressing myself into that region as if I can write only with the scent of its imprint on my skin. I don't dare write about myself. Instead, I depend on the eccentric characteristics of a provincial culture, creating gothic characters in the tradition of William Faulkner, Eudora Welty, and Flannery O'Connor. In the beginning this pleases me— *Why not a doctor with a wooden leg? Why not a matron who worries only about hats? Why not a daughter born on a riverboat docked in the Narrows?*—but in time I see this construction as a foil, a trick, something keeping me enclosed, boxed in, rigid, while more than anything I long to break free, to splash myself across the page. After all, I was born in a small Alabama town to parents who wanted nothing more than to live a middle-class life, to have mortgages and Cadillacs and Sunday casseroles, and I need to explain what happened to me in that little town. Explain the mysterious angst that wooed me away from their desired future, from what I came to think of as a predictable life. Explain the very thing we all want to explain: what it feels like to be me, to get under my own skin, to sneak past the official censors and reveal the hungry heart. But how can this be done? How can I write what I can't yet see?

I can't.

Instead, I put on a blue silk dress and rush off to work at Paramount or Universal or Columbia Studios, where I type dense contracts and rejection letters and angry memos, then eat yogurt and apples from the vending machine while my boss frets about the "Spic" maintenance men, the feminists "mucking up the act," the new dance musicals, "that goddamn John Travolta and Olivia Newton John." He doesn't talk to me exactly. I'm too much like the furniture, neutral and temporary, but while he vents, I watch him warily—not because of his political opinions, but because I'm anxious for him to leave for lunch so I can work furtively on my new story.

And yet that night when I walk out onto the roof, the new story clutched despairingly in my hand, I'm both puzzled and distraught because my character, Kay, won't budge, won't tell me what she thinks, what she wants, even whether she likes scrambled eggs or fried. She clings instead to some tired formula of predictable characters and vernacular language; though I close my eyes and try to evoke her, once again the hollow grate clangs shut in my head. Perhaps what I'm missing is the *real* story I have to tell. Perhaps my stories seem strained and contrived because I haven't found their essence, their soul. Perhaps I have to peel away another layer of skin. But how, exactly, do I begin to do that? How does any writer do it?

It's during this time that a fiction-writer friend of mine struggles through a bad patch in her life and leaves abruptly for Montana, a place as foreign to her as the moon. She's from the East Coast, with its private schools and Persian cats and manicured lawns, while Montana is all dusty cowboys, horses, and endless horizons. And yet it's here in Montana that her writing turns a corner, boomerangs to dead center. She calls to tell me that her life is indeed falling apart and all she can do is try to capture its descent, write it out as it appears before her eyes, pulsing through her fingertips like quicksilver in the dark. "I can't write fiction," she wails over the phone. "I'm sending you something to read, but I don't know what it is."

When I receive her carefully typed pages, I'm stunned by a piece of writing so uncannily naked, so bare of formal artifice, that I sit down on the curb in front of the post office to finish it. It's as if an afternoon shower has blessed a parched day, a wave of purple warmth flooded bare earth. As she falls in love with the West—her only reprieve from a broken heart—I fall in love with the narrator's intimacy and immediacy of emotion, the way she describes an erotic love left out to dry, its ankles thickening, its knees powdered with restless dust. Though I don't know what to call it, later I'll learn that what she's written is a personal essay, an autobiography, shaped and lifted out of the chaos of her life. What excites me is that it's a piece of writing that takes her consciousness as its core, digs deep into her character without a fictional disguise. I have never considered writing so honestly, so intently out of the grassy swamp of my own mind, but in one instant what's been unconscious is made conscious. I see clearly as if reading haloed words in the air: *Write about your life.* I know, of course, that it's not the events in a life that are important, but the assessment of those events, the astuteness of the writer's judgment, how consciousness is unwrapped, untangled, and revised . . . all in a fever of desire. And simultaneously, I recognize that I'm a woman in bondage to my past, a woman caught in a cultural web, a trap I've been unable to resolve in fiction for the simple reason that I've avoided the oppositions in myself.

Quickly, I get up from the curb and begin walking. I have no destination, no direction. Along with being excited, I'm suddenly frustrated, confused. I walk aimlessly past the known streets near the ocean onto a side road that leads to fields and fields of blooming wildflowers. Looking at those purple and white bursts of color, I try to puzzle out the scraps of my past. What I see is a young girl dressed in fashionable clothes, a girl who tries very hard to stay focused, on track, a girl prepped with good grades, dates to the prom, initiation in the National Honor Society, acceptance at a private college. For a moment I feel proud of that girl, hopeful and nostalgic, until with sudden clarity I recognize the flaw in this perception, the fly in the ointment, the storm gathering in my mental horizon. I see the girl shivering, trembling with anxiety, begging to stay home from school. I see the girl frightened of losing, the fear like a metallic hammer pinging rhythmically inside her head. The truth is that in adolescence I became terrified of failure and avoided its hot sting by pulling back, closing down, not allowing too much in. Oh, I gave all the appropriate noises of being in the fray, but in reality I'd given up, lost my nerve, and in doing so forfeited the capacity of experiencing myself.

Ah, so there it is: the ruptured girl, the frozen life, the seed of autobiography.

Stunned, I sit down in the middle of the field, lost in thought. If hiding was my earliest pivotal experience, then writing stories was my first act of self-discovery. Unconsciously, I chose the one place I would not be able to hide. It was a single act of courage, a leap of faith, my attempt to write about the place that had strangled me, and yet here too I limited myself, found a groove of performance and settled in, closing off questions while remaining dissatisfied, knowing my stories didn't quite ring true. I see now that I relied on received ideas rather than primary insight, depended on traditional characters, quirky and rural, borrowed from the literature of the twenties and thirties, men and women who had no relationship to my life, clumsy imitations of stories created by great southern writers. I was indebted to a place and a time and had not been able to shake myself free of my mentors. Writing fiction brought me closer to experience but left me shy of the self.

After reading my friend's essay, I realize it's my own consciousness I need to confront. Perhaps by writing about myself I'll discover my identity. Regardless, I'll have to stare at the rough edge of sadness in my life, the thin blades of rage, the tough, stubborn pride that often evokes a stony silence. In my stories I've avoided sad characters, avoided the anger and self-contempt, the illusions and longings of those of us who have hidden from ourselves. But sadness, of course, is a necessary place that every life visits; for the first time I see I have a story to tell. The story of masquerade, of subterfuge, of a lost consciousness found.

Writing autobiography allows me to open up a vein of self-scrutiny, to investigate the cracks and splits of my life, peering through the slippery veil of what we call "character" to define my own peculiar subjectivity. Never am I so engrossed in writing as when I sense the past opening up in me, memories branching out into understanding as if a bright light has suddenly shined down on the tracings of an event. Though some writers cling to shade, protection, cover, others long only to skate to the center of the pond, to balance precariously on thin ice. There's something uncivilized about such a performance, something primal and shattering about a mind that prefers this effect, that prefers danger if only because danger is an erotic probe, a slippery noise. The attraction, of course, is to reveal to the reader that all taboos are broken, all bets off: There will be no deflection, no camouflage, no scrim of protection, though every autobiographer knows this is not exactly the case, for autobiography is as shaped and distilled as any other genre. And yet autobiography allows the narrator a kind of striptease, a virtual disrobing, the titillation that certain minds find thrilling. Intrigued by pain, the savage mind craves the taste of steel in the mouth, the unruly pleasure of the scratch, the bite, the scar, the solace of transgression. You might call it self-surgery and repair all bound together into one, for a savage mind is obsessed with itself, obsessed with its stigmata of shame, the intensity of its longing, and I believe, with the potential heat of catharsis.

But is catharsis the proper aim for a literary work? Is that not best left to therapy? Does the desire itself contaminate the literary process? This controversy has been raging in American culture since autobiography in the form of memoir emerged as a prominent genre. The argument insists that memoir is so much navel gazing, so much narcissistic indulgence, whereas the same ideas or characters transformed into fiction or poetry remain aesthetically vital. What I want to suggest is another argument for memoir, an argument based on the contemporary writer's need to locate the self in a transient world— not just the political world of the twentieth century, but the world of personal identity in conflict with constant change. The primary plot of our current memoir involves loss and estrangement, separation from the parameters of family, community, religion, and culture, the protagonist attempting to dissect not just the loss itself but the value systems and expectations that accompany such loss. Although the prevailing myth of the late twentieth century is one of social, economic, and political progress, the current memoir suggests a countermyth of private shame and disgrace, a narrative of breakdown and recovery, a spiritual longing for connection that goes unfulfilled. Often in the past fiction and poetry have diagnosed the culture's ills, have told the hidden story of those forsaken, mistreated, rejected, recounting tales of who we are and what we long for beneath our bank accounts and fashion statements. I suggest that an integral part of to-day's diagnosis is being written as well through our society's memoirs, its autobiographical essays of men and women who give shape to memory's conflicted desires.

It seems inevitable that before I begin my odyssey into autobiography, I will leave the confused, cosmopolitan landscape of Los Angeles for the pastoral farms of Iowa. In 1984 I drive across deserts and mountains to a four-square prairie farmhouse, a quaint, yellow, two-story house that looks as if it's been dropped into the middle of nowhere, with winter fields as its only close company.

It is November, the fields are bare, the sky chalky gray in a swirl of white. When I stare out the windows at the land, old corn stalks look as if they've been slapped at the knees and made humble, barn doors are bolted tight against wandering deer. Nothing moves here except the battering wind and crows circling a power line. And yet it's on a fiercely cold day that I begin writing my first personal essay, sitting in the upstairs room of the farmhouse, a black eye patch over one eye, my computer perched on a makeshift table, a mattress on the floor. Having gotten an eye infection while driving across country, I've come to this farmhouse outside Iowa City to recover and work. Now I hunch over the keyboard, leaning close because my perspective is skewed, and try to shape the stories of my adolescence, the beginnings of panic, the freezing of ambition, a subterranean anger that finds no openings into air. I've never talked about this time in my life, and yet as I type, I feel a key turning inside my brain, a spirit that opens me wide as if a door has blown loose and wind rushes in. I have so rarely felt this accompaniment that I'm transported to another existence. Words pour out in startling sentences, paragraphs, pages, until there's nothing left but a pleasant quiver in my wrist. Ghosts of the past rise up to be blessed and scorned; they settle like defiant, anxious children to be reborn.

When I finish the essay, it's late night, the sky bright with stars. I want to remove my eye patch and read what I've written, but I know my eye will weep and flinch at the light. Instead, I hear the dogs bark and go downstairs to let them out, tiptoeing past my friend asleep on the couch. It feels good to step alone into the night air, with its clean slice of wind, its moon troubled and thin. Everything here is so different from the busy clutter of Los Angeles. Up above the barn bats swoop and dip, and I turn toward the dark finger of road that divides the land. With my one good eye, I take in the flood of emptiness. With my one good eye, I begin to discriminate the sharp edges of the fields, the clear outline of a distant barn, the shadowy husk of a tractor. With my one good eye, I look intently at myself in the world.

WHEN THE HOUSE BEGAN TO TREMBLE ─────────

Laura couldn't believe it when I told her I was writing a book about myself, squealed when I told her over the phone. "*What?* That's a lovely case of insanity!"

I laughed. It was perhaps the best description of autobiography I'd ever heard. To write a book about yourself, you must want very badly to understand a relationship that seems inexplicable, one that is not only lucid and intimidating but also opaque and defying. You have to be a little crazy.

"Who are you going to go after?" she asked. There was relish in her voice as if she'd just conceived the idea of blood.

"Nobody," I said.

"Absurd."

"Not really."

"Sure it is. Writing's a war. You're always doing somebody in."

I said politely that I was examining the mythologies I'd grown up with, assessing how culture changed with each generation. "Autobiography," I continued, "is a resource of creative self-examination, a way to—"

"Rubbish," she interrupted. "It won't be any good."

In some ways Laura was right. Autobiography, like fiction, must engage in a war, revealing the plight of equal contenders with something urgent at stake. That's the classic structure of fiction: conflict, complication, and then resolution, with the conflict setting up and defining the war. In autobiography the war is often a fight between parents and children, and the shape of the battle is whether the child can ever get free.

Free of what, of course, is the question.

In my forties I began to write a memoir about my mother and myself. The words didn't come easily or simply. They seemed to take years. From childhood I'd watched my mother from the sidelines—the backseat of the car, the frame of her dressing room door—and from very close up when she let me touch her hair or watch as she put on Chanel #5 perfume. She was very dark, very pale, her hair a raven black, her throat so white it reminded me of lace. As she tucked me in bed at night, I thought her beautiful and imaginative—she told wonderful stories—even though she rarely smiled. Joy, if it came, burst out in a frenzy of busyness, a quickening of interest. "There's so much to do," she'd say if she got excited, especially when that excitement involved buying new clothes—which surely had to be altered or fixed—or finding a teacher for the talents she wanted us to have. When she was pleased, she frowned with such intensity, I often mistook it for worry. But then the frown softened and she hurried off to cook another meal, teach another class, mail another package at the post office.

And yet what I must tell you is a discovery. What I wanted all my life was to tell my mother to stop. Just that. I knew, without understanding why, that busyness was a deflection and beneath her hurry and bustle lay a pool of rage, a fury so thick, so hot, it would burn at the touch. To avoid it she collected shoes and lipsticks, taught biology and Sunday school, wrote diets for the hospital, visited foster homes and nursing schools, wrote recommendations and thank-you notes, cleaned the closets and the refrigerator, cooked gumbo and baked pound cakes and whipped up lemon meringue pies. She ate standing up, better if it was a peanut butter and banana sandwich washed down with a Coke, a piece of cake pinched off as she picked up her keys. She woke every morning with her hands clenched, went to sleep every night as if she'd fallen into a black hole. I used to imagine that the inside of her head looked like a tilt-a-whirl, everything in motion, circling and swirling, high-pitched screams muffled by the constant grinding of the gears.

What she wanted, I think, was immunity from the world's harshness, its critical glare. What I wanted was immunity from her world, from her critical gaze. But, of course, that was impossible. She was my mother and I called every week. A dutiful daughter, the one she had groomed. Busy. Tense. I woke with my fingers cramped, a fist beating inside my chest. I rushed from city to city, clocking in ten cities in six years, carrying my stuff in U-Hauls all over the country, eating peanut butter crackers in Holiday Inn bathrooms, then quickly getting back on the road. I took the family pattern to heart—became a whirligig of motion—and yet all the while, I wanted what she desired for me: to be a successful middle-class girl.

But as I began to write my memoir, I saw that I had failed to become the kind of daughter my mother had wanted, failed at middle-class girlhood and the southern lady standard, failed to achieve the status I was expected to achieve. How had this happened? What had I become?

During this time of writing, my mother and I took a trip together to Cambridge to visit my niece at Harvard. It was my mother's first trip to Massachusetts, her first visit to Harvard, and while we waited for my niece, we settled into our hotel room, relaxing to our own comfort zones. I lay on the bed, cloaked in dimness, while Mother stared out the window at a side street where people walked quickly through the soft slush of newly falling snow. Having lived all her life in a small Alabama town, she was surprised by the foot traffic in this sudden winter storm. "I wouldn't walk out there alone in the evening," she said, her brows knit together. "I don't think it's safe."

I stood up beside her, watching the pedestrians in their varied paths.

One man lifted his face to the snow and opened his mouth, tonguing its wetness. A woman hurried past him, never once glancing up. Teenagers streaked by in long, baggy flannel shirts. No coats. No hats. They laughed as they raced each other down the street. "It's in the middle of Cambridge, Mother. It's probably just fine."

"I still wouldn't do it."

It was the dead certainty of her fear that surprised me. It reminded me of her response to my first art studio in California. The studio was a large two-room affair in a working-class neighborhood with a generous sprinkling of ethnic groups and artists, men and women who often bantered as they walked—and sometimes fell drunkenly—down the street. "Remember when you visited me in Los Angeles? Remember how afraid you were to cross the street?"

Mother frowned. "It's because of where you lived."

I nodded, knowing the neighborhood looked shifty, bedraggled. And yet once you stepped inside the studio, a trapeze dangled from the ceiling, its sleek silver bar glittering in the afternoon light. I could climb up on that bar any time of day or night and swing out into open air. It was like flying. Like dreaming. Like diving into outer space. Just by closing my eyes I could propel myself into a whole new life. Beyond the trapeze were work tables, drawing tables, desks, books, a darkroom, art supplies. The ultimate work space for an artist. Secretly I'd thought my mother would be pleased, since work was the driving force of her life, the primary value she'd bequeathed to me. "What about when you came inside? What did you think of it then?"

"I thought you must have been depressed."

Depressed? I was stunned by this comment, by the certainty of her words. "What do you mean? Why did you think that?"

"Because to me," she paused, "outside presentation is an expression of inner worth."

I started to protest, to resist, but as suddenly my world cracked open. I glimpsed what had eluded me for years: My mother mythicized work as the means to middle-class presentation while I hungered only for work that would transform me. In a single instant I saw the conflict in our ambitions.

Now I smiled at her. "I wasn't depressed at all. In fact, it was one of the happiest times of my life. Didn't you know that I was living the life of an artist, the life I wanted to live?"

"No," Mother said, equally surprised. "I didn't think anyone would want to live like that. You had nothing."

That night I lay in bed, listening to the soft purr of the heat whispering through the vents and the muted sounds of Friday night traffic. Mother was asleep on her side of the bed, a blanketed blur beneath the covers. I thought about her childhood in that bleak mining town in northern Alabama, where kids slept three or four to a bed and the only beauty was the blood-red sunset that transformed the slag heaps into rough black hills. Coal dust covered everything, clung to her clothes, powdered the white sheets on the clothesline, settled in the deep red-gullied ravines. Couples crammed nine or ten kids into a company-owned house where the family's prized possession was an upright piano no one could play, and the kids' only rewards were the good marks they made in school.

The house I grew up in held antiques and Oriental rugs, thick white bath towels and closets full of good clothes. The kitchen had every type of device a modern cook could desire—a Cuisinart food processor, a built-in grill, marble pastry boards, an electric coffee grinder, an ice maker, a blender. Beauty and taste and symmetry were everywhere. Every year my family acquired new upholsteries, new lamps, new cushions, new clothes to replace what was no longer fashionable. And yet in my dreams at night that house began to tremble, to sway and flounder, to totter like a foggy-eyed drunk. Sometimes dresses loosed themselves from their hangers and rose like ghosts into the air, flying out the windows as the house groaned and shuttered. Other times the roof exploded and the furniture—the lovely Louis XVIII desk and the upholstered linen sofa, the chandeliers and dining room table and chairs—was catapulted skyward, drifting aimlessly toward the stars. In my dreams I was always outside, watching, waiting excitedly for what would happen next. I knew that I was witnessing more than the destruction of my mother's careful selection of beautiful objects. I was seeing my own willful defection as well. I was leaving that house. That life. Even in these dreams, I knew I'd made this happen, and always I woke feeling both ashamed and relieved.

And yet it wasn't the house I was defecting from. It was the ambition of that house. The desire to take up the art of accumulation, to live a middle-class life.

What I couldn't tell my mother that day in Cambridge was that I had lived in that house like a hungry ghost, uncertain of my desires and ashamed that my ambitions seemed so aberrant, so doubtful. All my life ambition had been a marked word, a screaming word, baring its teeth. At its mention I'd tense and tighten as if something dangerous had been said. "I want you girls to have ambition," Mother used to announce as we drove to music lessons past fields of harvested soybeans, past the Corte's barn and the gladiola sheds on the east side of town. Birds flew above us in the sky. Even they, in their formation, seemed determined, inspired. I knew my mother had left that mining town at age sixteen on a work scholarship to the University of Alabama and never once looked back. Getting away from poverty, from physical abuse and the ugliness of the mines, was the catalyst for her ambition. As I stared at the flat, endless fields, the kudzu ditches, the stiff, rigid blue line of the horizon, I used to wonder what would be the impetus for mine.

The next day my mother and I walked down Charlestown Avenue toward Au Bon Pain, where we were to have coffee with my niece. It had been raining intermittently, the snow melted, the skies gray and sullen, cars splashing water against the curb. All around us were crowds rushing past, the mishmash of conversation and noise, the bustle of a city street. Then in the middle of it all, a little girl started dancing in her tights and coat, twirling and wiggling with abandon, her many braids flying. For a single instant the crowd stopped, admired this extravagance, then rushed on, the little girl smiling, then grabbing her mother's hand, walking on.

"Well, somebody's having fun," I said. I watched as the little girl pulled on her mother's arm, then was lost in the crowd. "I wish I were dancing, don't you?"

Mother looked away from me at the shops we were passing. "No, I was never a good dancer." She frowned. "Probably because we weren't allowed to."

"What do you mean?" I asked, curious, bewildered. I thought of her family as big and noisy.

A sudden gust of wind blew through the trees, and we stopped for a minute, buttoning our coats. "Oh, you know," Mother said, "anything that was fun in my family was considered *sinful,* a waste of time. Growing up we weren't allowed to dance or sing or do anything like that. If we danced in the house, my father said, 'Stop that foolishness,' and you better believe, we stopped. If other people had parties we weren't allowed to go."

"Even when you were in high school?"

Mother looked embarrassed as she often did when I asked too many questions about her past. "Oh, honey, I wouldn't have gone anyway because I didn't have any clothes. I had to wear Mrs. Elgin's old shoes to school. Brogans that didn't quite fit."

I hadn't known this. I thought of all the times I'd watched my mother getting ready for parties, dressed in an evening gown of chiffon or silk and beaded high heels for balls and dances where couples did the fox trot and the two-step, sometimes the cha-cha-cha and the waltz. "But what did you do for pleasure?"

She looked at me with surprise. "Why, nothing. The only thing I learned to do was work." We trudged on down the street, silent, watchful, each caught in her own private thoughts. Work, I thought. *Only work.* The insistence of it secretly infuriated me, irritated me. Suddenly I wanted to break out in a run, but of course, I didn't. My mother had a bad hip and I made myself slow down. "Pleasure still makes me feel guilty," she whispered as we came in sight of Au Bon Pain.

And inside me something stopped.

What I remembered was the first Thanksgiving I'd spent in Los Angeles, the year I'd left Alabama. That week my friends in the art department buzzed with plans, with trips home to New York and Pasadena, to San Diego and San Francisco. "Gotta go to the P's," my best friend Julie sighed, but I knew that secretly she was thrilled at the idea of going back to New York. A few people were having a potluck in L.A., and another friend, Scott, invited me home with him to Laguna Beach, but to each group I said no.

"Oh, do you have other plans?" Scott asked.

"Yeah, I have to work," I said.

"*Com'on,*" he said. "Who are you kidding? It's Thanksgiving!"

But I held firm. I knew my family wouldn't question my motives. Everything in our lives was deferred to ambition. Work alone was sacred, gave you legitimacy, allowed you eccentricity. As a family we were a mere generation away from poverty, from miners and maids and fishermen, people with no means other than back-breaking work, people who were abused and sneered at, people with poor posture and bad teeth, people who lost hope and took to drink. Though my own family might have good clothes and furniture, might speed through the dusk in a brand new car with leather seats and automatic windows, we knew it could all be lost in the dark. What kept the car moving was us. Though my mother and father had moved from the working class to the middle class, I know now that it takes three generations for a family to secure its place in a new class. Class, that precarious indicator of who you are, is not as mobile as we've been led to believe. For the first generation there's nothing beneath you to shore you up, and the insecurity of that—those working-class grandparents with their overalls, lunch boxes, and rough shoes, and the hard climb of the parents—breeds in the next generation an insecurity about caste. Only in the third generation is there a sense of entitlement, a feeling of middle-class ease.

That morning I woke and dressed as if it was any other day of my life and drove to UCLA. The art building was a six-story structure just off Sunset Boulevard. I had a key to the building, but what I hadn't anticipated was just how deserted the entire campus would be. I walked through the sculpture garden, past the Rodin and the Henry Moore and the Miro, aware for the first time of the emptiness around me. Above me sparrows wheeled through the sky, merging then separating. Squirrels scampered up the trees. Nothing else moved. There was not a single person on this part of campus but me. I hummed to myself in the elevator, whistled as I opened the door to the studio where I'd be working. Again, silence, a husk of a room. Other people's projects were spread out on tables, pushed up against the wall. Cindy's smock was still hanging on her chair.

I got out all the paints and dyes I'd be using, the scraps of cloth and paper. I intended to experiment, to let my mind roam free. But instead of expanding, my mind seemed to contract, to whittle itself down to the narrowest point. I heard my mother's voice. "I can't stand failures. There's no reason to be a failure." And I knew this was the implicit story within a familiar code: You must not allow "life" to interrupt your ambition, to derail success. You must shut off the siren calls of the body, seal yourself off.

I opened up the paints, mixed the dyes. Twenty minutes by the wall clock. I painted over the orange design, deepening the shade to red, then decided I hated it. It looked like a bleeding cross. Twenty more minutes. I put that away, picked up some black cloth for reverse dying. I painted a primitive design in wax and soaked it in bleach. While I waited I stared at the clock, watching the second hand click slowly around the circle. I pulled the cloth out of the bleach, thinking it needed another layer of texture, something circular or spiral, then decided it wasn't worth it. I worked for another thirty minutes, listening to the noises of traffic out the window, the drone of the refrigerator where we kept our dyes. But it was no use. I couldn't seal myself off. I thought of all my friends sitting down to an extravagant meal, the insignificant chatter, the fuss over the turkey and cranberry sauce, and on impulse, I rushed home to call Scott, to see if it was too late to go with him to Laguna Beach.

As I rode in the front seat of his car, past the outskirts of Santa Monica and Venice, past the closed shops and sun-swept driveways, I felt guilty. I knew I had failed. I couldn't work, I couldn't . . . but then, at the crest of one of the curves, I caught a glimpse of startling blue, a rush of white, and everything that had been sealed up inside me broke free. "Oh, look!" I said as if Scott had never seen the Pacific Ocean.

Only much later did I understand how different passion is from ambition. Passion places no emphasis on the future, cares nothing for external validity, is internally driven, sustained by intuitive desire. More often now I trust people who tell me they *must* go to South America, *must* canoe the Upper Peninsula, *must* read Austen or Gass or Faulkner, but have no rational reason as to why this thing must be done. It simply must! Desire comes from some unconscious place. It was only after I moved into the studio and began working on autobiographical art that I understood passion. It alone could bear me beyond my awful anxiety, my inherited demands. It alone gave me permission to fly.

In my dreams I never let the house totally collapse. I stood outside in the wet, spiky grass and listened to the wind in the pines, the swishing of needles high above my head. I watched the house with a clear, focused beam as if my eyes had become my mind, enhanced by a singular vision. When the house began to sway, I felt excited, entranced. I was safe in my voyeuristic destruction, thrilled when the curtains billowed out the windows and lace tablecloths and linen bedspreads floated by in clouds of white followed by evening gowns, wine glasses, and round sterling silver trays. *There! I wouldn't have to be a hostess.* On other nights the house shrank, squeezing itself tighter and tighter, excreting the laundry, the dishes, the refrigerator, and the stove. *Wa-la! I wouldn't have to be a caretaker.* My favorite dreams occurred when the house rose from its foundation as if spirited by desire. It hovered six inches above the ground as if paused in the middle of a dance. It was no more rooted than I. No more stable or defined. The house was in motion and it too could choose to say good-bye. It too could change its ambition. It might swing out on a pale silver bar and vanish in the night. Or it might remain, transforming itself, becoming taller, darker, as round as the moon.

As I think about that trip to Cambridge with my mother, a place we chose to be together, I realize that Laura was wrong. Autobiography's intent must not depend on exposing the foibles and perversions of another person, skewering someone for her flaws and eccentricities. Instead, autobiography must show how relationship becomes conflicted, how the patterns of desire can be thwarted by our very human failings. In my own case, it was by writing a memoir that I came to understand my mother's need for middle-class ambition and to respect that desire. Now when she tells me about redoing the dining room or the commercial success of one of my peers, I can be happy, knowing that such things bring her pleasure. And she continues to surprise me.

"You're so happy with your life," she said to me the other day on the phone. "I always listen to you because you know what you want."

I laugh because it's not entirely true. My dreams are just as ambitious as my mother's, and just as slippery. Neither of us will get exactly what we want.

"I'm happy enough," I say and realize it's true, that each of us defines our own slice of happiness. After we say good-bye, I walk out to my backyard and begin pulling weeds from among the flower beds, pulling up the creepers that tangle in the roses, the juniper grass that is crowding the hostas and ferns. Across my lawn I notice the sun-flowers just beginning to bloom, their stalks like long, fragile arms bent over the fence, the blooms a burst of yellow, the center a thick, velvety black. The entire backyard is a flood of late afternoon sun, the grass a startling green. On impulse I fling off my shoes and leap from my spot in the shade into that golden warmth. And here I stop for a minute. I stand absolutely still.

A PLACE AT THE TABLE _____

I read once that Annie Dillard said you must write down the nerve of
your obsession. Unconsciously, I've always done that, written close to
the bone, near the hidden trauma of my life. But recently I discovered
something troubling about myself, and this discovery, like all discov-
eries, has been both painful and prophetic. It blew in like a typhoon
on the raging wind of writer's block. Suddenly, this summer, I could
not write. When I sat down at the computer, my mind went numb as
if stunned by the very presence of itself. Ideas swarmed inside my
head, but I couldn't translate these ideas to images, couldn't give them
dramatic form. I'd write a paragraph, then stop, looking out the window at my neighbor's laundry, taking a peek to see how their underwear was doing. Relieved to see that theirs too was gray and stretched,
I glanced back at the words I'd written only to feel winded, as if I'd run
a marathon, though I'd barely managed a few sentences. Before long
nausea set in and I didn't bother with the paragraphs. I simply avoided
my study and did laundry myself.

But why couldn't I write? Or, as I began to translate the question,
what induces me to write, to push through confusion to definition?

This question perplexed me, and though I'm not finished with it,
I came to understand something about my obsessions. I discovered
that my passion for writing—for distilling and dramatizing stories—
emerged from a sense of anguish, a feeling that something "unseemly"
was thrust deep inside me like a painful thorn. I had to get it out! Dig
down deep and exorcise the hurt. I had to make sense of it, grab the
dirty roots and bring them into the light. Getting it out was not just a
matter of pride—as if an old enemy was standing right around the
corner, snickering at my bad luck—but a fundamental need to clarify

what was painful. That required interpretation, a leaning away from the hurt to see what lay behind it.

If anguish has been my *I Ching,* my North Star, guiding me to new ports of call, it wasn't an anguish born of simple indignation, but a more complicated condition: the confluence of love and fury. Fury alone sends me into spasms of self-destruction, days of hiding in bed, eating too much or too little, ridiculous declarations ("I'll never speak to Sharon again!"), but when fury is attached to an intimate relationship or a revered place, it works a different sorcery. Now I must not only understand it but transform it. Now I have to give shape to the thing festering inside me, tell its story, evoke its characters, resolve its conflicts. Only then can I jump up on my sofa and dance.

Most often this anguish circles around my origins in the rural South, a place of swamps and lagoons, of creeks and bays, a place where people still say "honey" and "chile" and "sugar" and "girl" as if they're the most natural words in the world. It's also here that I learned that cultural training can be denounced and rejected, but its shadow remains coyly in place, ticking like a time bomb. That is what held Quentin Compson captive in Cambridge, what confused Julian in "Everything That Rises Must Converge." All of Eudora Welty's characters in *Delta Wedding* must contend with the conflicts of heritage, with the tensions that arise between insiders and outsiders, the unsettling of that smooth weave of the upper class. It's a well-known premise that early training in the narrative of place is what most southern writers wrestle with, quarreling and sometimes communing with the abominations of a class-driven, race-haunted culture tied to the false legitimacy of a lost aristocracy. But this is not all that I, as a writer, must wrestle with. I also wrestle with the love, a primitive blood love, a contorted, gut-wrenching sense of belonging that is irrational and fundamental, as mystifying as it is pleasing. That's the killer, this love I have for the physical place and for the mores of a people whose lives so often vex me that I turn away in incredulity and shame. And yet beneath the shame are these words: *my people.*

I think of a friend who married young and went to live with her husband in a little bitty trailer, no bigger than a camper. "Right next to us was a scrap yard surrounded by a chain-link fence and guarded by the skinniest dog you've ever seen," she said. "I mean, he looked anorexic, like he wouldn't have the energy to chase you away if he wanted to." My friend tells me she was learning how to cook that first year and loved mixing things together—the carrots and the squash and the sweet Vidalia onions from a farmer's market—but everything she prepared, her husband disliked. "So guess where it went?" she asked. "That's right. Poor dog got fat and lazy. So fat the owners moved him to another part of the yard and I couldn't even feed him. Thank God, I finally got the hang of fried chicken and turnip greens." And I see my friend standing in jeans before a puff of flour, a rope of light coming in through the window as she breads the chicken, listening to the hiss of grease in the skillet, wondering if the glory of the world is as simple as a meal. If only she can get it right, then in bed each night she might not have to forget herself so completely, lose the angles of the day, the slip and slide of ordinariness. Even as she thinks this, she sees the dog lying by the fence, its tail wagging, its bony haunches jutting through tight brown skin, and she feels a moment of gratitude so surprising it stuns her to stillness.

In many ways I am like that woman. I keep trying to get the stories right, working alone in my cramped mental space, hoping to please both myself and those who matter to me while the hungry dog gets fatter and fatter on what must be thrown out the door. And yet, like that woman, I trust the value of the ingredients, the ordinariness of my experience, the pleasure of the task, knowing that getting it right is the goal I long for. If I can give voice to those people who live inside me, then I too will have grown larger. I will have set a place for myself at the table.

* * *

For a long time I thought it was only fury that prevailed in me. At age twenty-six I believed I could exorcise the South by an act of will. I would simply leave and re-create myself, strip away what had been unconsciously grafted onto me so that new ideas could attach themselves with impunity and purity. I was an innocent then. I didn't know that ideas are not as simple as spores, that ideas—no matter how appealing—cannot be welded to a mind, that ideas are not iron-clad rules to hold on to but elastic boundaries you shape bit by bit. Of course, what I really wanted was to change something fundamental in myself, to make myself into a "self," a woman worthy of praise and admiration, someone interesting to take along on the trip.

Since I had no idea how to do this, I left Alabama on a hot summer day before the dew had evaporated from the velvet green lawns and the heat slapped its scolding message into my bones. Dressed in a tank top and jeans, my car loaded with clothes and notebooks and art supplies, I drove to Los Angeles. Here I would become someone different—and always I imagined that difference startling not me, but the folks back home. After much rushing around, I got an apartment, set up housekeeping, started graduate school, and yet, like a boomerang, once I left the South, I became southern. I said "*Juuu*-ly" and "*perrr*-fume" and *supp*-pose," putting the accent always on the first syllable so that people turned automatically and smiled indulgently at me. "You must be from somewhere *else*," they said.

"Aren't we all," I replied, but I felt caught, rebuffed. Wasn't this a make-believe town?

For weeks I walked around as if I had a mild concussion, my brain stymied by the southern contention that "a girl must be nice," as if acceptance in a big city was grounded in generosity and acquiescence. When landlords hung up on me, I said, "Oh, I'm sorry," to the dead phone, then very carefully put the receiver back in its cradle and stared at my freckled knees, wondering what I had done wrong. When I worked on a political campaign and the manager asked me into his office, explaining that he expected me to do well in the canvassing because people responded to blonde females with soft voices, I took this as a compliment. I smiled. Only later did it occur to me that this was a sexist comment meant to encourage stereotypes.

When I walked down wide boulevards where mansions were hidden behind hedges, where hibiscus and bougainvillea crowded the entrances, where the horizon was one clean blue line, I saw instead dirt roads, the red dust rising in clouds, the wheels of a truck bouncing in the distance. Doves flew in squadrons from their perch on the telephone lines. A shimmer of mosquitoes hovered over the ditch. I stood in the middle of a busy sidewalk in Westwood and analyzed the sky. It seemed all wrong. Too flat, too blue, too intense. Where were the fleeting scraps of clouds? Where was the yellow-rimmed horizon? Where was the fog that wrapped so tight around you you became a ghost? Where was the familiar social network I had felt so conflicted by?

What I had hated, it seems, was proximity to the very things that had formed me, like a tomato plant that hates the dirt and the sun. But once I recognized love not as invasion but as obsession, I stood up in the sun and the dirt and said, "Mine." Love, it turned out, wasn't the soft slipper of loyalty I had believed it must be, but a conscious curiosity that beat deep inside me, a continuous throb of pain and pleasure I was forever seeking to understand. What *was* this place I was from? And how had it shaped me?

I began to think of the small-town South not just as "that awful place I had to leave" but as a passive-aggressive adolescent coached by its parental figure—the Northeast—to become normal: profitable, industrial, aggressive. To remake itself in another image. The image of progress. And yet, in my own mind, it wasn't normalcy the South needed but prophecy, eccentricity, and the faith to reckon with its own abominations, the misjudgments of the underdog. What I wanted was for the South to clean up its act, to stretch its imagination away from the pragmatic goal of fiscal stability and "good times" and toward a quieter goal of moral discrimination. I began to think of the South as I might of an artistically talented student whose parents demanded that she become vocationally trained in college with a degree in business. This student was competent to do such a thing and felt duty-bound to comply, and yet her real growth and creativity came through the humanities, through wrestling with paradox and perspective, with interpretation of theme and structure, with the context of words in a sentence. It was through wrestling not with "fact" but with fiction that the metaphor for achievement proclaimed itself, and achievement meant the making of internal cohesion, the moment of insight, wisdom, clarity. What I wanted from the South was a maturity of vision, not the influx of wealth and prosperity, not a dance partner with fancy shoes.

Having finally understood this, love for place seized me when I least expected it to. I remember a visit in late March, a day of standing on a pier in southern Alabama, feeling the sweep of the wind against my face, the smell of brackish water, salt and seaweed, the taint of dead fish and moldy barnacles. I looked down at the drift of water, the splash of waves, then back at the horizon where gulls pinwheeled across a white sky, and felt that shiver of desire. *To be here. Only here.* It came unbidden. A visitation.

The more troubling and oddly redeeming aspect of writing for me is that word fury. I don't think of fury as toxic. Instead, it's a resource, a wake-up call. When I feel fury, I settle down, become very quiet, very intent, pushing away the cloud of doubts that strangles new thought. Incensed, I'm like the spine of a book, holding together my entire conflicted history. It was confusion that made me leave the South, a sense that, having grown up in my particular family, I had to conform to a contradictory code of feminine behavior, a set of terms that utterly baffled me. In my parents' attempt to raise girls who could make their way in the professional world as well as the domestic world, I was trained to be both competitive and nurturing, confident and self-effacing, ambitious and nonassertive, friendly and inaccessible, flirty and asexual. Perhaps this is not so different from the training of many girls brought up on the cusp of the sixties, girls who would negotiate two distinct and troubled worlds. And yet all these categories left me so confused I knew nothing to do but run away.

I left with no politics except the politics of escape, fueled by a mantra: *Get out, get out, get out.* I knew nothing about feminism, had learned my lessons about female life inside my family and on the way to the Dairy Queen to get a Dilly Bar. It was here that I watched the older girls in their pedal pushers and middy blouses paired off with boys in white T-shirts and khaki pants. The girls teased, whispered, and seductively licked their ice cream cones while the boys attacked their banana splits and slapped plastic spoons on the Formica table in hard, fast rhythms, their eyes blazing with curiosity and anger and something I couldn't yet name. They threw paper napkins at the girls. Tried to snatch their ice cream cones. Flipped toothpicks and slapped pennies. The girls wiggled, pinched, playfully pouted. I knew this was ritual, the oldest dance in town. But secretly, I was afraid I wouldn't be able to get the hang of it. Secretly, I worried that flirtation wouldn't be my realm, and flirtation ruled much of the discourse of the South, the nuance of play and pleasure. Secretly, I knew that I hadn't been brought up for pleasure but for something more flinty, more engrossing, possibly damning. Even as a young girl, I felt the pressure to creep out to the periphery and look back at the journey I'd taken, not just to look at it but to diagnose its worth, both to me and to the world.

Even as a young girl, not knowing the world, *I wanted the world.* More than the sweet hum of pleasure, I wanted the battleground of ideas, the slap and hiss of argument, the sweet moment of revelation. But I could never have said this back then. I could only whine and complain that I didn't fit, that my life in the South was a mess, a failure, a breakdown waiting to happen. I could only leave and by leaving stake a claim.

And yet fury, I believe, has kept me alive.

It is a muggy day in Los Angeles, the kind of late December day that makes me long for an honest-to-God winter—snow and ice and difficult driving—something I've never really known. But it's near Christmas and I'll be going home to Alabama very soon, exchanging one mild climate for another. In southern Alabama the days will grow thick and dreary with coastal fog brought in by a southeasterly wind. The landscape will look soggy, draped in a costume of gloom, the skies flat gray, the air thick with water, even the pine trees and magnolias and water oaks bleak against a muck of red mud. But this holiday, I think, will be different. This holiday I'm bringing home my partner, the man I've been living with for six months, the man I will marry. For the first two days I delight in showing him around: the long flat ribbon of road I biked as a child to Magnolia Springs, the hidden springs themselves, then the shrimp boats, the wide, flat plateau of rivers that interrupts the marsh, eventually winding their way to the Gulf of Mexico. Here are the canals where alligators hide in summer, emerging occasionally with the swish of a tail. Here are the estuaries. The farms. "And see all those soybeans!"

All around us, my family is busy with the business of Christmas—decorating and baking and shopping—and it's not until that festive day is over that my father leans toward me one night as he takes off his shoes.

"I don't know what to tell these grandkids about you two living together," he says, looking directly into my eyes. He stretches his feet. "You know only white trash do that here, and we think it's immoral."

I'm not surprised by this comment. I've already had this conversation with my parents over the phone, have felt the force of their disapproval in both words and a restrained silence. I've told them what I know to be the truth of my life: Having gone through a bad divorce, I'm frightened.

And that's what I say to my father now. "Well, Daddy, tell them the truth. Tell them that some people get burned in marriage and don't know if they can make that commitment again. Tell them you don't approve, but there's nothing you can do."

"You can't tell a bunch of kids that!" he says, his face flushed. "They think you're doing something wrong."

"But we're not," I say, getting excited too. "We're *not* doing anything wrong. It's just an old set of standards you're living by." But, of course, this is the very issue. Who makes the standards one lives by?

As always my father and I are stirring something up, getting to the juice of our lives, though neither of us persuades the other of the validity of our points. It seems, in fact, an abstract argument, yet one that brings us closer to each other because it's at the center of our lives. "You're a hard case," he says to me that night, but still he bunches his lips for a kiss.

"Good night," I say, both relieved and worried that we always argue.

A day later I'm riding with my sister down a familiar highway to Lillian, not paying much attention to anything but the wildness of the land, the way the trees look sepia toned in the late afternoon light, their leaves a brush of darkness against a salmon sky, when suddenly she says, "You shouldn't do this to my kids."

"What?" I say, surprised at her comment.

"They don't know what to think of you living with someone. And you act so self-righteous about it too."

"That's not true," I say, defending myself, and yet the old feelings of being "not right" return. Instantly, I feel embattled, gloomy. At that moment my sister *is* the South, the voice of conservative propriety and indignation, entitlement to community support and respect. Sitting in her car, I know that my leaving *was* a flight for my life. But alongside that feeling is another more urgent one, the first surge of anger, the desire to even the score, validate my own sensibilities, a demand to be heard. It's here that I burst out of my old cocoon—the one that had no politics—and come alive, splashed with the fire of rebuttal. It's here that whatever has been sleeping in me wakes up.

This is the moment I will come back to again and again when I write. Not this literal moment between my sister and me, but the symbolic moment of conflict: a child of a region confronted with her transgression and disfavor now ready to respond, to take that leap of faith in her own conception. It's here that imagination whispers. It's here that I listen to what I have to say. The act of writing is an act of recovery. A reenactment and revision of all that went before. At least, I believe, that is the goal, the one good meal.

I am looking out my window at my neighbor's laundry. The underwear sags and drips. Again, I am pleased, relieved that the fullness of life takes its toll on our most intimate things. It's a small moment, I know, but it reminds me that I'm not as agitated as I was a few days ago, not so certain that there's nothing left to say. Now I think about the pleasure of exile, the way my life has twisted around a place but has also grabbed hold of new roots and strengthened its grip. I stand at the window and watch the soft greenness of the Iowa summer, the way the trees bend in the prairie wind, the bursts of sunflowers, their centers like dark satin eyes, the soft trellis of leaves on a neighbor's arbor. I do not look for the storm. I know that it will come and surprise me. I know that I'll turn my face to it and be swept into its fury. I know that I'll become engrossed, soaked to the skin, falling deep into its reverie. This is the way writing happens. And you wait for it.

The personal essay is dead, the "I" evicted from the fashionable venues of literary nonfiction. Or so I've been told.

"The world is just *sick* of people writing about their lives," a colleague complains to me behind the closed door of my office. He is clever, wry, visionary, and I feel myself shrink as his eyes make a panoramic sweep of my desk, where pages of a memoir lay stacked in a disheveled mess. I think of what I've written there, how my family hacked our way out of poverty and nailed ourselves to the middle class, the spikes digging deep into the marrow of our skulls. I think of my mother, who saves string, my father, who prefers to eat in the kitchen, my aunt, who says, "Ain't that right, honey?" when she wants to acknowledge that the world is a rough and perilous place.

"Think about it," my colleague says. "All that narcissism, all that unresolved emotion."

When he leaves, I briefly worry that my writing is irrelevant, old fashioned, tied too fervently to fury, to self-obsession, to the complicated issues of class. Perhaps I have no right to material so close to me, stories that fester and clot inside me like the beginnings of a chronic disease. Perhaps it is passé to write about the struggle between temperaments, the duel of consciousness within a family. Perhaps the old way of storytelling in the essay is dead. Now it's time to be experimental, sexy, to jump on the bandwagon of the new, new thing, those essays that intimidate and confuse, essays that threaten the rest of us to see them with uncritical awe.

"It's better if it's a little more obscure," a student responds in class to an essay about a young man's relationship to his father. "If it has gaps, you know."

"Yeah, we need to unpack it," another student agrees. "That's what we're supposed to do . . . figure it out, you know, like unpacking a box, not being sure what we've got, not being sure what's really there, only what we *think* is there."

I see myself yanking out conflicts, tossing out reliable narrators, letting them wobble and shudder to a stop.

"The more fragmented, the better," the first student says. "Then it's one discourse pitted against another."

Well, maybe, I think to myself. But these are merely the buzz words of academia, and such words—so easily misunderstood—often have little to do with the success of an essay, the clarity of the thinking, the hills and furrows of a meditative form, the ability of the writer to engage the intelligent heart.

But what is the intelligent heart and who gives a fig about that anymore?

Sometimes I think I sit alone in my room, in a solemn universe of me and like-minded friends to whom I can point and say frankly, "We care. We believe in the intelligent heart!" We believe that personal stories matter, that whether autobiographical or cultural, the story must act as a catalyst for thinking and feeling, that it is the congruence of both that elevates the essay to the status of art. The intelligent heart is the heart that seeks revelation in dreams, then turns dreams into insight, and insight into wisdom. The intelligent heart is the balance beam, the quivering tightrope we walk when we dip perilously into our psyches and gather up the stray bits and pieces we patch together and call art. Perhaps, more often, the intelligent heart is a masquerade, a carnival, a devilish trickster we wrestle with constantly, fighting shadows and phantoms in our attempt to find its true shape. Not that its true shape will give us any peace. Its true shape merely defines for us the oppositions we can work with, the strands of ambivalence we hold up to soft morning light. When functioning properly, the intelligent heart knocks at our door, awakens us from dreams, shudders from the drafty places in our apartments, and demands a quick audience. *Write this,* it says. *And this. And this. And this.* Faithfully we write it down, trying to quiet the alarm that it will be embarrassing, stupid, irrelevant, or that most insulting of faults: already done. We listen because it is urgent, because it sneaked up behind us and blithely tongued our ear. We listen because it seemed hungry and furious, as alive as thunder before a late summer rain. We listen because we know that stories come from the mystery of knowable places, the slime coating the muscle of an oyster, the brine of a shrimp, the tough thready strands of a tangerine. We know that everything we receive—*even this, this summons*—must be untangled and distilled, worked like the unraveling of rope, piece by piece, thread by thread, then put back together with the embrace of two broken thumbs. The intelligent heart is no mere bud of ornamentation. The intelligent heart is the source, the goods, the first principle from which everything else is made.

But this is not to say that the intelligent heart is all. Should anyone demand this, I would rise up in protest and draw my sword. "All" is something that can't be defended, dictated, enlisted, tabulated, or decreed. In every piece of good writing is something suspect, a shadow lurking in the corner, a stray hair fluttering across the page, a drift of wind, a low fog that obscures the promise of understanding. Every piece of good writing has trouble, the quirks of personality and temperament, the dizzying graduations of self-love. No, the intelligent heart, in the end, is something elusive and longed for, the thing that can't quite be attained. The real problem for most of us is that the intelligent heart often remains buried for years, letting us grind out bare, quixotic but emotionless forms, forms that please our cerebral betters, that thrill grant committees, that delight bored academics. These are forms that grow hairy with stylish weight but that live, we secretly know, because of lack. And there is safety in lack. Safety in style. There is even, I admit, a kind of awe.

But when all the huff and puff of fashion slips away, the safe, stylish essay, cooked in the safe, stylish brain, is nothing but a husk, a fancy dress, a decorative facade covering an unknowable story, a secret life.

"Nobody wants any more of those personal stories," my colleague says. "Who cares about the I? Who cares about the woman in the storm? The family drowning? The mother clawing her way out of filth and dreary disease? Who cares?" he asks.

But I don't bow my head. "I do," I say, gathering up the pages of my story.

I refuse to be dead.

INSIDE MY SKIN

Once I had a blind student who thought I was an Amazon.

"You sound big," she said. "Are you tall? Are you fat?"

The students around me laughed. "She's skinny," one of them said. "A Twiggy with more hair."

It seemed a pretty accurate description, though I was surprised that I sounded big. I always thought of myself as small, even in tone, but realized if you can't see, you must imagine people by the sound of their voice, the lilt and sway of their cadence, the power of their words. Those of us who are sighted notice other differences: skin color, class, beauty, age, and physical disability, to name but a few. If the blind student could have seen me, she'd have noticed that I'm a white, middle-class, middle-aged woman with blonde hair and blue eyes and no obvious physical disabilities. Had she been sighted, I wonder if she'd have made different judgments about me. Would my voice have seemed as powerful to her? Would she have focused instead on the nervous habit I have of jiggling one leg while sitting at a table or smiling broadly when I come into a room?

I don't know. But I do know that by the time I had been writing autobiography for several years, I longed to step outside of my own cultural sphere, outside of white, middle-class America, where I felt both an insider and an outsider. Though I'd grown up in the middle class, I left that financial security in my twenties and didn't return to it until my forties. I lived, I guess you might say, outside the domain of class, being both a student and an artist. Then in my forties, I joined the ranks of academia and have remained there for many years. What I couldn't step outside of was race. To be white in the places I've lived is to be in the majority, the dominant population group. And yet what strikes me as most pertinent about this dominance is how seldom I've been aware of it.

I think now it was merely serendipity that I happened on V. S. Naipaul's essay about Tuskegee, Alabama, while living in Iowa in the early nineties. As I read, a kind of electric charge went through my body. I was from Alabama and I'd never even been to Tuskegee. Though I was living in the Midwest—and had been living here for several years—I knew I was going to make that journey to Tuskegee. It was an emotional decision, not an intellectual one. What compelled me, I think, was the unknown and the unknowable. I didn't know what I thought about race. And yet intuitively I knew that being in the minority rather than the majority would make me live deeper inside my skin.

I wanted that. A wake-up call.

A dark night, a clean, clear night when I stand in the brightly lit room and examine my whiteness: My face is as pale as the moon, my eyebrows a wisp of smoke, my lips barely touched with pink. Freckles speckle my nose, my cheeks, and with one finger I trace the veins along my forehead, thin tracks of soft, faded blue. Sometimes I think I can lie on my bed and disappear, a ghost-self of near invisible hue. "You're just so . . . *so white!*" people yell at me on the beach, laughing at my absence of a tan. At such times I blush, embarrassed, turning quickly away, but tonight my whiteness tells a different story. It shoves something old and forbidden down my throat.

I'm staying in Tuskegee, Alabama, a small historic town in the Black Belt of Alabama, a town whose population is 99 percent black, a town I never visited during the eighteen years I lived in Alabama. No white person I know went there either, as if Tuskegee was another country, a foreign land, a discarded place that existed on the far side of the moon. But now, at age forty-six, I've interrupted something in myself, walked over the border and put down my suitcases, shaken the dust off my shoes. I've come here intentionally, done all the things that intentional travelers do: checked air fares and schedules, made arrangements for a place to stay, rented a car (my getaway), bought a new shower cap and extra toothpaste, and worried about what I'm trying to find. It's not that coming here is so radical—this visit to an all-black town. No, what astonishes me is that it's so deliberate, so purposeful, so fraught with foolish expectations and hungry dreams. Like all travelers, I've come here to translate myself, to become someone different, someone new, as if the journey itself is an act of transformation. And yet I'm frightened. I don't know how to act, how to treat black people as friends, as equals, as part of the casual conversation going on inside my head. In my mind, their history keeps them separate, distinct, like guarded souls sealed up in a story I have no right to, a story of public pain and hidden pleasure, while my story stems from hidden pain and public pleasure, the fate of a white middle-class girl.

But those first days in Tuskegee, I don't see any of this. It will take me a long time to understand that what frightens me has lived all along inside me: the terrible fear of being unmasked, vulnerable and disappointing, a girl with too little to hold. Awareness shimmers only in the distance like heat lightning flickering on the horizon, the air too close to my skin. Instead, I stare at my whiteness in the mirror and wonder, *What can I possibly hope to rectify?*

"We've got to *rectify* what we've done to the colored folks," my great-uncle used to say as he drove me through the narrow streets of his small Alabama town, staring out the window at the black men who sat together on the courthouse square, exchanging gossip, dipping snuff, watching the white folks go about their daily business. They looked older than Moses, their skin the color of ash, the whites of their eyes as milky as an oyster. My great-uncle's skin was the color of Vicks vapor rub, brown-spotted, wrinkled, mottled chicken flesh loose at his elbows and knees. "Yes sir, got to rectify," he nodded, earnest, sincere, though I could tell he hadn't a clue what rectification might include beyond the Civil Rights Movement of Dr. Martin Luther King Jr. Though I nodded in agreement, I had a lot of other things on my mind, things like love and happiness and a particular man named Thad. Oh, I applauded all the right causes—integration, civil rights, affirmative action—but I had no intention of changing my life for them. Ideas were ideas. They lived in the cool isolation of your head.

Though I saw little of my great-uncle after the beginning of the Civil Rights Movement, I remembered how vigilantly he stared at the TV when Dr. King was on, turning up the volume and pushing his glasses up on the bridge of his long nose so he could see "that black man tell 'um how it is." I was older by then and too busy with my own life to attend to my great-uncle's, as little by little—like a turtle—I pulled my head out into the air. I sniffed the winds, took stock of the direction of other people's thoughts. I married Thad and worked for the Department of Public Welfare in a small Tennessee town, spending a good bit of my day going on home visits, trying to ignore the chickens that pecked around my feet in the scratchy dirt yards and the hound dogs that rubbed their mangy backsides against my bare legs. There were as many poor whites as poor blacks in the county where I lived: sharecroppers and scrap haulers, maids and cotton pickers, trappers and junk dealers. "Can't you help get me no job, Miss Pat?" a woman would sometimes ask, looking appealingly at me with dark, anxious eyes, a child clinging to her arms, but I was too busy with paperwork and time sheets to do more than issue food stamps and send women to the Health Department for pregnancy tests and birth control pills.

"Sorry, Ailene, you have to go down to Mrs. Turkle for that."

What shook me up instead was that my own life fell apart. Divorce. Breakdown. Unemployment. I had something to rectify then. It wasn't just an idea. No sir, it was like redirecting the flow of a mighty river swept into some wild, serpentine path. The water chilled and terrified me, sweeping me along in its mad, unruly flow. Rectifying, I realized, was a heap of trouble all its own.

"Yes, ma'am," the maid says with bland politeness when I ask for extra towels.

"I don't know why I use so many," I continue, as if I need to explain myself. I'm still in my old blue bathrobe with the frayed collar and want to say something nice to this neatly dressed black woman in the gray uniform, something more personal about why I'm here at the Conference Center in Tuskegee, Alabama, about the writing class I'm teaching at the library, but what is there to say? When the maid leaves,

I sit down on the bed and sigh. I've been here two days and everyone is so polite, so formal, it's like a stone wall of resistance, everybody nodding and smiling, their smiles frozen, predictable, like the smiles of clerks in Kmart—*have a nice day!* I worry a loose thread on my robe as I finger the extra towels. I had expected it to be so different, to find myself immersed in the soft chatter of talk, as if talk had a size and shape big enough to roll around in, to get lost in. Talk is what I came south for, believing it would be an opening, a wedge, a movement in the brain like the hiss of rippled silk. When I sped down the interstate on Wednesday, high on purple wildflowers and air thick as gauze, I thought of this as my big adventure, a kind of prodigal return. "Carrying on," I imagined my great-uncle saying, nodding his earnest approval. "Yes sir, *rectifying.*" But now I'm cautious, self-conscious, like a person on display. I've never been so aware of my whiteness before, my blonde hair knotted in tight curls, red lipstick accentuating the paleness of my skin. Maybe it's the wrong color. I get up to wipe away a blur at the corner of my mouth.

Stop worrying, I tell myself. *Quit this fretting.* "You're just getting your feet wet," I say to my image in the mirror. And it's true. I've come down here to teach a two-day summer writing class to men and women at the public library. It's an idea I dreamed up myself, a belief that writing will bring people closer to themselves, closer to each other, as if writing is the great liberator, the freedom bus, the healing tonic close at hand. To calm myself I sit on the bed, practicing relaxation exercises, filling my mind with gentle black faces beaming their good will, their pens poised above sheets of clean white paper.

The class meets in a small storefront library, one shabby room with a life-size poster of Zora Neale Hurston and fewer books than my own library at home. Twenty people sit crowded around three tables, staring at me as if I just dropped in from Mars. I'm surprised to see two white people, a white woman and an elderly white man who sits erect and separate, tufts of cottony hair sprouting from his ears.

As soon as I'm settled in an empty chair, the librarian, Mrs. Louisa Dawes—a pretty caramel-colored women dressed in bright pink—raps on the table to quiet everyone. "Y'all, listen now while I introduce Miss Foster, who's come down here from Iowa with a P. H. D." She says each letter as if it's separate and important, and immediately I think I should be smarter, wiser, more poised than I can rightfully be. And yet the class looks unmoved by the announcement, as if Ph.D.s are as common as dirt, no more bother than a dog's breath, a flea bite, a spider's web, and I tell myself to settle down, get with the program. As I move to the head of the table I see the assignment I asked Mrs. Dawes to distribute last week sitting undisturbed, on top of the stack, and I have a small but cataclysmic panic attack. *What am I doing here? Who are these people?*

I look over at Zora and I swear she winks. *Com'on, girl. Get a little action going.* And I move quickly to the "getting to know you" phase of the class.

"My name is Carter Johnston," the first man announces, rubbing his hands together as if he's about to throw lucky dice, "but everybody calls me C.J., so you can too." I nod hello and we go around the room: Miss Carlene, Miss Xaviera, Paul Z, Mrs. Roberta, Mrs. Bessie, Miss Cicely, Miss Lasanya, Miss Corinne, Miss. . . . Men and women anywhere from thirty to seventy years old, three girls no more than sixteen. Despite my desire to pay attention, I'm distracted by a piece of paper fluttering near the air-conditioner vent. It sounds like the buzz of a small helicopter, like a mind splitting apart. I notice a fly zigzagging around the group, circling and circling as if it's gone mad.

"I'm excited that so many of you have come to the library to write about your lives," I say, though my voice sounds pinched, self-conscious, and quickly I move to a fifteen-minute pep talk on concrete detail and specificity—"*Now when you talk about a hat, you've got to tell us whether it's a blue ball cap turned backward on your head or a wide-brimmed sun hat with pink ribbons unraveling in the breeze.*" I plow through the field of my knowledge, spouting familiar ideas that grow like alfalfa in my head: character, dialogue, point of view, dramatic situation, diction, exposition, interior voice. I'm off and running, feeling suddenly exuberant, purposeful, words slipping easily off my tongue as I talk about the way a writer slows down the narrative to show a particular moment, an action, an event, a thick slice of life. *The moment of horror when you watch your dog run out in front of a car. The moment you see your sister dive off the pier into the swampy creek. The moment you wake up frightened from a bad dream.* As I settle into my spiel, I greedily collect the heat of their attention like a single focused gaze—*they like me!*—a loosening among us, and I'm relieved that I'm able to ad lib, to settle back down to earth. I'm in the middle of a sentence when a white hand shoots straight up like a spear in the air.

"Yes sir?" I'm pleased by a first question.

The white man leans intimately toward me, brow wrinkled, lips pursed. He swallows loudly as if there's phlegm in the back of his throat, then says hoarsely, "Now listen here, you're doing all the talking. I don't like that. What makes you think you have so much to say?"

Too astonished to reply, I only nod at him while something old swells in the back of my throat. *I am nothing, no one.* I look beyond him into what seem like black expressionless faces: One woman is quite beautiful, her tight gray curls sculpting a small, regal head; another woman looks tired and bored, sucking on her bottom lip. One girl pulls at her eyebrows. Another twirls her dangling earring. An older woman picks lint off her T-shirt, which says in bold letters ADVANTAGED. There's an awkward pause and I realize I've misinterpreted their interest. They were merely being polite.

"Well, she's the teacher," Miss Carlene, a large black woman, speaks up. "She's *supposed* to talk." Miss Carlene smiles benevolently at me and with that heat, blood flows back into my veins. I give Miss Carlene a private room and extra bath towels in heaven.

"That's right," I say as if this is news to me. "I'm supposed to talk . . . but I'm only introducing the subject, and I want to hear from *all* of you, so let's get down to the business of writing. Let's write for fifteen minutes about a moment in childhood that still has heat, a particular event that's filled with emotion, then we can *all* talk about what we've written."

Though they begin promptly, heads bent, pencils moving, all but three women stop writing after five minutes and stare blankly at the dust floating in the air. "I don't much like writing," Miss Cicely whispers when I ask her what's wrong. "It don't come out like it's supposed to."

"I can't think of nothing to say," one of the teenagers says and begins erasing.

"I'd rather read stuff in a book," C.J. agrees, looking expectantly at me.

But, of course, I've planned nothing of the sort, have stayed up late thinking only of writing assignments until they've multiplied inside my head. I frown at the clock. Two more hours to fill.

"Well, I don't know about the rest of y'all, but I want to read my stuff," Miss Carlene says proudly, then stands and reads a story about being invisible, unseen, sitting out on her front porch under God's blue heaven and vanishing like milkweed in the air.

"That's wonderful," I say, grateful for this woman's lush, honest voice.

"But she ain't white," C.J. says. "Milkweed is white."

"I don't think it has to be literal," I say, smiling. "It can be representative, symbolic, something blowing away, vanishing, you know."

"I don't think it works," C.J. persists, looking archly at me.

"You don't know anything," Miss Carlene says. "Listen to the teacher."

"I went to college longer than you did," C.J. says. "And I *know* it don't matter if it's concrete if it's *wrong*."

Somehow we manage to get through the next two hours, the air conditioner blasting us with frosty air, the men and women bickering with each other, some not bothering to write at all, but chatting with each other while I talk. At the end of the class people say their goodbyes, telling each other about the Saturday market on the square, about the revival going on down near Notasulga every night. "You oughta come," Mrs. Dawes tells me, "and see what it's like." There's the scraping of chairs, the sudden wash of heat when the front door's opened wide. I see the old white man look insistently at me, demanding my attention, and for a moment I think he'll apologize as he sidles up close and leans near.

"I hope you *learned* something today," he says scornfully in his loud old man's voice.

Alone in my room, I marvel at what I've learned: First, this is no adventure, no blessed return. Second, nobody likes me. I can feel it in their eyes. I'm just a drive-by visitor dumped in their laps. And writing? How could I possibly have thought writing made anything clearer? Writing is just plain hard. It stirs up the water, makes things murky, cloudy, unsettled, all those ideas jiggling fast against each other, shaking loose fuzziness instead of focus. I'm so upset with myself, I get in my rental car and drive to the next town, a white town, where I can sit in a restaurant and look bluntly at white people, not caring a hoot what they think. I listen to the chatter of other customers, hear the waitress joke with two old men in the next booth. "Oh, I'm hanging in there like loose teeth," she laughs as she refills their water glasses and asks about their golf game. Then she sees me and smiles sunnily. "Now what you want, sweetie?"

What I want is to understand why I'm here, to believe it's not all vanity, indulgence, some old karma working its way through my mind.

Slowly, I eat my hamburger, then drive back along the winding roads, past the old Victorian mansion with intricate fretwork, a small windowed turret, and a spacious porch that wraps around the west end of the house. Once it must have been beautiful; now sun-bleached weeds grow wild near the entrance, and peeling paint and busted screens suggest desertion. A dead raccoon lies stiff as a stuffed toy in the middle of the road. Kudzu drapes over trees and ditches, and when I roll down my window, the air feels like Jell-O. I swear it hasn't moved all day. Even the trees look wilted into place. I drive past the boarded-up windows and faded Dr. Pepper signs in the town, and when I go through the lobby of the conference center, I stare straight ahead.

The next day only six faces greet me around the table. Six black faces. The white people have fled. Good riddance, I think. Maybe it's the whittling down of the class that makes the difference, but today I'm more pulled together, not so anxious or afraid. "Let's talk about race," I say, looking at those six curious faces, "about the fact of it, about the stories we tell ourselves about it, about the silence behind it."

Miss Carlene vigorously nods her head. "I can't *stand* it when somebody says they don't see color. Everybody sees color. It's the first thing you notice."

"Absolutely," I agree. How smart I've become in twenty-four hours! Only yesterday did I realize how white I was. "But good white people don't want to admit it. It makes us nervous, makes us think we're racists and we don't want to be racists anymore. We think we're liberated, been given our exit papers."

Miss Carlene smiles. "You know, when we left here yesterday I asked these girls if they had a moment of forgetting that you were a white girl . . . just a moment." She pauses. "And you know, everybody shook their head. You are just . . . *white!*" she laughs. The girls start to giggle and then everyone joins in.

As we laugh, the tension eases out of the room as if it's a bad smell that's been hanging around us for days. My shoulders loosen. My mind clears. Everything seems ready now, poised for my assignment, the one I've been waiting to give. "Everybody can write about our difference," I begin, "the distance between the races, but I want you to write about a moment of intimacy, of emotional closeness you've had with a person of another race."

Xaviera's mouth falls open.

"Nah!" Roberta scoffs.

"I can't," Cicely whispers, pushing her chair back, frowning.

"No, I mean it," I say. "A 'moment' of intimacy—not a lifetime. I just want everybody to think of one time when you've felt something about somebody of another race. Maybe you admired something, felt sympathetic toward somebody because they were sick or in trouble, or maybe you've helped someone or they've helped you."

Six black faces look at me in dismay. "Maybe you don't know the person well, but you've noticed something about them. You know, you see a woman who's having a hard time carrying her child or a man pushing his Down's syndrome kid in a swing." I'm backpedaling now because there's so much resistance. "You see someone in a wreck, a little kid who's fallen off his bicycle, an old man in the emergency room." Truth be told, I'm also having a hard time thinking of examples; what comes to mind isn't intimacy with a person of another race, but the feeling of intimacy I had for my great-uncle when he made his pronouncements advocating change.

"I used to think I was better than black people," he told me one Sunday when I brought him some crowder peas my mother had put up in the spring. "Thought it meant something when a black person stepped off the sidewalk when I walked by. Stepped right off into the dirt, they did because they had to. I used to think that was the way it should be. But that was only an immature ego, something that made me feel better, kicked me up a notch. It was the way I was brought up, thinking color not character made the man. Character . . . now there's something to think about. Then one summer I worked with a black man up at the university. I was shelving books and he was emptying the trash, but he'd read more than I had, and when I had to open up the Special Collections Room for him so he could get the garbage there, he asked me if I'd read Faulkner and Tolstoy. Said they'd make me think about things."

I can see my great-uncle buttoning up his old cardigan sweater and picking up a watering can, going out to the garden, talking to himself about Sutpen in *Absalom! Absalom!*—*"Jesus, all that naked fighting in the barn and that business with Clytie"*—or about the worms on his tomato plants. I thought when he talked he said important things, things my family never talked about, as if certain silences were the natural order of the universe. In silence there was protection and safety in which no mistakes could be made, no danger spread. Silence meant there was no arguing, no indecision, no bad thoughts leaping from your mouth. But silence also meant there was no unburdening, no sense of relief that the worst part of you was pushed out into the air.

As I look at the class, I realize I've seldom said what I think about race because I don't know what I think, except that black people make me feel anxious and awkward, as self-conscious as a mole startled by sunlight. Even as I sit here I remember the evenings my mother and I drove through Aronville, the black section of my hometown, with its shanties and wide ditches, its septic tanks and dead snakes lying like discarded belts in the road; I'd shrink at first from looking at the houses, the people, the dirt yards, as if an aesthetic barrier protected me from this community. Though the sun still shone like a faded orange bloom in the sky, everything here looked gray, dirty, sunken in, the porches warped, rickety, sometimes an entire house leaning at an odd angle, the cracks in the doors and windows covered with cardboard, nothing but wooden stilts between the house and the ground. It was obvious even to a child that any critter could work its way into the foundation, and I knew that rats and snakes would most likely be first. If it was summer and we were taking Ora home, there would be the smell of collards and pomade and something sickly sweet mixed with the smell of dirt and goldenrod and honeysuckle. In winter the smell of wood smoke, pine needles, and burning leaves dusted the air. As we drove by, skinny-legged black children stopped in their games and stared at us as if suspended in a vision, sticks and balls clutched tightly in their hands. Simultaneously, I'd stare back at them, trying to assimilate this world into my picture of American small-town privilege with its black maids and yard men, its trips to the ocean, the swimming pool and shopping malls of Mobile. I knew I should smile at these kids, but I was simply curious, wanting them to show their distress while they merely stared back at me as if I was an anomaly too.

For a moment I sit quiet, listening to the air conditioner start its wintry blasts, thinking how we've all just claimed the racism in ourselves.

"Listen," Roberta is the first to break the silence, "black people can like you, but you can only get in so far," she says, holding her hand about two feet from her chest.

The others nod.

"But that means you can never really let a white person be your friend," I say, withholding the word "me."

"That's right," Roberta says. "That may sound bad, but it's true. What happens over a lifetime of bad things happening is you don't allow yourself to trust. You get mean and small. There are decent people on both sides, but when you've been through as many battles as I have, you've been worn down."

"That's it," Nancy chimes in. "And there are days I take offense at what a white person says just because I'm in a *mood*." She looks sad, dispirited, not happy with this truth. "But you know what would kill me? If my son married a white girl. *That* would be a betrayal."

At first I stiffen as if rebuked, but then I think of how often I've heard the same sentiment from the other side. Nothing terrifies many white people like the threat of intermarriage. It brings up the possibility of black babies and kinky hair, of a solid line dividing the family into two tribes. And yet as the talk continues, it surprises me to discover that most of these women have a white person in their families, somebody "married in," somebody from up North, somebody crashing the party. For a while I remain quiet, but then I say, "You know, if I'm honest, I've never had a moment of intimacy except with the black maids who used to work at our house. That was all I *had*."

They nod at me as if now I've entered their world. The world of color. The world of buttressed lives and blunt talk, the world of stalled separation, of stark memories. "That's the only good connection my auntie had," Xaviera says. "She was a maid to these white children and she was always talking about them. Once she came home and told us about fixing them blueberry cobbler and how good it was, how everybody put whipped cream on top and the little boy ate three helpings. She was so proud of her cooking. But I hated that little boy because I didn't get no cobbler. But I don't want to write about that."

Just a moment, I think, and realize how presumptuous I've been. Instead, we continue writing about our childhoods: Carlene argues with her nappy hair, Xaviera with her chubby eight-year-old self. Louisa mourns the loss of the country, the real country with polecats and wild dogs and moonshine hidden in the woods. Roberta surprises us all by writing about a can of syrupy peaches she longed to eat. *And there was only one left, sunk deep in the bowl, buried by an ocean of syrup. I reached in to pull it out. So sweet. So good.* When the two hours are over, we don't stop, but keep going until Carlene throws down her pen. "Okay, that's enough. I've got to have me some carbohydrates."

Someone goes across the street to Syder's Grocery, and we push back our chairs, waiting, then heaping vanilla ice cream and strawberries in plastic bowls, cramming our faces, laughing and talking while the ice cream melts in a puddle of sugary cream.

That afternoon I drive away from Tuskegee, looking at the white sheets blowing in the wind beside a house trailer with a TV dish larger than the car. I see tarpaper shacks falling in on themselves, vines climbing smartly up the telephone wires. Black children run around the yard, yelling, playing some game. As I drive farther into the boonies, I think about the story my great-uncle told me about a visit from the Ku Klux Klan. It happened in a small town in the mountains, a poor part of the state where he first started as a doctor. The men, mainly sharecroppers and small businessmen, waited with everyone else in the waiting room, staring at the picture of a doctor standing next to a little girl with polio. In the picture, the doctor and the little girl are both smiling, the little girl with leg braces and a snaggle-toothed grin, the doctor modestly proud. The men remained until the last patient had been treated and left, then stood up as a group and said their piece. "We ain't sick," they said. "We're just here to talk. Business." And they made their offer while sweat leaked down their backs, and their necks strained with expectation. The doctor would be a catch. An important member.

But no, he shook his head. "Got lots of sick people in the county," he said. "That's enough to keep me busy." No anger. No *Get out of my office*. No threat to stop this foolishness. The great-uncle just picked up his black bag and walked out to his car.

"Got to rectify what we've done," he kept saying to me. "Got to act." And I'd imagined white people going into Tuskegee like an army of Peace Corp volunteers, nurses and teachers and plumbers, taking with them everything they'd learned. But so much of what we've learned is the bare fact of color, the blunt paternalism of power.

In the dusky light of early evening, I'm sitting in a dark parlor, looking at the ravaged body of my great uncle. He's lost in old age and illness, moaning occasionally, then coming back to himself. I listen to the rhythm of the white housekeeper chopping onions, preparing dinner. Behind her the sky is slate blue, the cicadas just starting their nightly drone. I begin telling my great-uncle about the trip from Iowa to Tuskegee, about the students in my class, how we've talked about the nuances of race. I hide everything that's been difficult, uncertain. I don't tell about my own nervousness, the way anger and tension rise in me like a tide. I don't tell him about my uncertainty, my confusion over what it means to be a good person, a good white person. The old man listens for a while, then waves his hands in great agitation.

"I can't hear about that. There's no more time," he says, his voice so quavery I go quiet and still. "I gotta talk to Jesus." And he closes his eyes. "I love you, Jesus," he whispers in his faint, quivery voice, and when he opens his eyes, tears bud on the lids. For the first time I notice his skin is sallow and dry, the color of old sandpaper, the veins faded and prominent, big bruised spots flowering like tiny eggplants across his hands. The cicadas buzz louder, shriller than a chorus. He coughs and spits, then he points a finger at me. "Who are you? You the teacher?" he asks suddenly, as if he doesn't recognize who I am. "You the one with big ideas?"

I nod.

"Carrying on," he says with a hint of a smile. "That's the thing to do." But so much talk seems to tire him, and without another word he closes his eyes, settles suddenly into sleep.

As I drive back to Tuskegee, I think that I no longer know what it means to carry on. I've come down here naive and ill informed, believing I could survive on good intentions. But good intentions never anchored anyone, never won any wars or established a beachhead. Good intentions, I understand, are among the passive virtues, safe conduct only in the landscape of dreams. Instead, relationships are built on mutual needs, often singly, one by one by one.

I try not to think about my great-uncle as I sit with Louisa Dawes in the African-Methodist-Episcopal Church in Tuskegee the next Monday night. I have missed the revival week of New Testament celebration, but I'm here for a baptism in this fine red brick church of over one hundred pews. Louisa invited me the last day of class and I surprised myself by saying yes, though it meant a quick turnaround trip to Tuskegee. So here we sit side by side in the middle of the church, surrounded by hymnals and programs and the nods of prominent members who sing with the spirit. The baptismal party crowds together at the very front of the church, everyone dressed in white, the women in white robes and hats that look like old-fashioned pillbox hats, the daughter young and soft in white silk, her hair pulled back into two smooth plaits braided with white ribbons. The minister talks in a voice of pure honey about losing oneself in life, about loss and resilience, about the very difficult matter of faith. I listen as he tells the story of losing his son to leukemia, about the real fact of grief and its anguish. I listen as he tells about a morning of demonic agony when he couldn't quit the sorrow, couldn't bless the life, then months later another morning of cool breezes and the smell of honeysuckle in the air, the chirping of birds, the first hint of relief. I watch as the little girl mounts the stairs to the baptismal, her legs like thin brown stalks. The girl vanishes from sight as she winds her way up the hidden stairs. Then she reappears with the minister in the balcony of the church, a place lighted with soft lights as if it's the very top of heaven. It's here that the baptism will take place. It's here that the minister holds the girl in his arms, asks her about her belief, asks her to choose Jesus, then lowers her whole body into the pool of blue water. "Take us to Jeeee-sus," the choir sings soft and swaying, as if singing is their life. "Give us to Jeeee-sus." And there is something in that pure sound, that lowering of a girlish body in a pool of cool water, that opens me. I feel a sudden spill of tears, and for once I don't try to tidy my emotions but let them leak across my face. I know that I am right in the middle of a difficult matter of faith. I don't know what I believe, what I want to believe, what I believe I can want. My great-uncle is dying and with him many of my naive notions of change. I don't know what will replace them, how I'll break this new silence. I'm caught in the middle of this when Louisa's hand moves over to gather up my own. It's such a simple gesture, I don't think as our fingers intertwine.

As I'm driving away from Tuskegee, I imagine a distant time in the future when my great-nieces will tell this story, repeating bits and pieces of what I've told their mother. They'll huddle together as little girls do up in the attic or the basement of one of their houses and talk about the old aunt, wrinkled and weird, the one who can't shut up about her stupid life.

The Last Essay on Southern Identity ———

"There was a time I was pushed to the river and didn't intend to jump," Ora says, pressing her hands tight together, then dropping them flat to her lap. "It was that gas man who did it. Came round here every week to check our meters, then started showing his privates, trying to get in the house at my girls."

Ora looks beyond me at a wall of pictures, little black girls in pigtails with snaggle-toothed grins, their faces open and trusting, white Peter Pan collars circling soft, sloping necks.

"He kept trying to get in, but my girls locked him out. They just sat real still and didn't say a word till I got home."

Ora sighs, telling me she was at work at Miz E's, cleaning for the family, doing the kitchen, the laundry, changing all the beds, pushing away all those cats. "When I got home they told me the story, and next morning I told Miz E, told her I'd been pushed to the river and didn't intend to jump. Miz E went right to the phone, called her husband and the po-lice, and it was taken care of." Ora straightens in her chair, her starched blue denim skirt crackling as she leans forward. "But I bought me a rifle, Pat. I wasn't gonna have nobody hurt my girls." She gazes beyond me at the pictures on the wall, shudders, then closes her eyes. "But he didn't come round no more. Miz E took care of it. I knew she wouldn't stand for that kind of behavior. She always stood up and said what she wanted. But I kept the rifle. Used it too."

I settle back into my seat, staring at Ora, then at Jesus on the cross two feet from my chair. An evangelist is shouting on the radio, then crooning in a soft, southern voice, "With Gooooodddd, everything is possible. Everything, my friend."

I think of the rifle. I think of Jesus. I think of Ora sitting as prim and proper as any antebellum lady, and I feel a jangling of the nerves, a ripple of excitement. I'm back in the South. Back with the women I love.

It's 1997 and I'm driving down a dusty blacktop, past miles and miles of weedy pasture, blackberries and kudzu growing from ditches wide enough to build a house in. A spread of light cuts through my window, warming the length of my thigh. I look from side to side, waiting for something, anything, a bird, a possum, a movement in the trees. Then I see it, a burned-out house, its tin roof sliding quietly, effortlessly into the dirt. A gust of fear prickles my shoulders. Abandoned houses. Ditches. Shanties. I'm out in nowhere, in a place I don't belong. I'm going to Ora's house in what we used to call "colored town."

"You come on," Ora said when I called earlier this morning. "I be here all day, so you come on."

Though it's been over forty years, I still see Ora sitting in the backseat of our Cadillac in 1956, a sack of greens in her lap, her head turned toward the window, her face moody, distracted, as if she's burdened with thoughts so distant from mine there's no way in. Her eyes flicker at the ditches like a horse ready to bolt. I watch her furtively, curiously, her body so rigid I dare not touch it though I sit right beside her, my knee wedged up against one of her sacks. And yet there's something I want from her, something that has to do with the right questions and the complicated answers, not the easy, paint-by-number kind. The questions I know how to ask go something like this: Why do they live here, Mama? Why doesn't Ora have a nice house? And why are black people so courteous and respectful to us?

Mother looks away, frowning at the evening sun. "It isn't fair the way it is," she sighs, glancing toward me, singling out the permissible question, "but Ora doesn't make enough money to live in a nice house. You have to go to college and make a good living if you want nice things. That's just the way the world is." I try to put Ora and college in the same thought—Ora strolling across the green lawns of a college campus with books in her arms—but she slips silently, effortlessly out of my grasp. This, of course, is the simple answer, ignoring the facts of the color line, implying that this is just "their condition," something intrinsic, inevitable, unremarkable, just the way things are, the way things have always been.

But I know it isn't so. I know as Mother drives Ora down the dirt road past the familiar shotgun shacks, past houses covered in fake brick siding, past Folgers coffee cans blooming with gladiolas and petunias, past the smell of collard greens and wood smoke, that whatever poses for reality is a big fat lie; later I'll understand that the underclass is politically determined, a ready workforce of cultural pariahs, sustained by custom and primed for obedience, but as a child, I know this only through feeling. *Ora shouldn't have to live in that house.*

It would be foolish to pretend that I've figured out the questions as I drive this morning toward Ora's house or that I understand precisely the anxiety of my position. The only thing I'm certain about is that my discomfort also resides in me, a woman who's had a hard time claiming a southern identity, a woman who's drowned too often in the quicksand of her own failures, flailing and squirming, sometimes begging for help. And yet I've always had the choice to pursue these failures, to wander aimlessly or tenaciously down my desired path. Now as I buzz down the highway to visit a woman who's had few choices, my own life looks plump and privileged by comparison. For a moment I think of myself that way: I roll down the electric windows, peer through the windshield of my fully paid-for car, and smell the dust as it rises from the sides of the road. Cotton plants thrust their thick, white blooms into the air. A cow turns its mournful head toward me and moos in dismay as if the sky might fall. In the thick heat of the day I'm released from my anxieties; I am going to visit Ora and I wonder what she will tell me about her life.

When Ora emerges from her house, she's slumped, a little shrunken, her grizzled hair smoothed back in a pageboy. She hugs me to her thin, spry body, neat and prim in a blue denim skirt and blouse, her feet in white tennis shoes laced up tight. I pull back, looking into the clear darkness of her eyes. She drops her gaze and says, "You Pat, you came all this way from Iowa." But before I can answer she's staring beyond me, her face alert, expectant. "Where's Miz Foster? Didn't she come with you?"

I tell her Mother stepped on a nail yesterday. "Wearing those thin-soled shoes and it went right through the ball of her foot." I can see Mother hobbling around the kitchen, pouring boiling water into the pitcher of tea, her face flushed, her foot in a pink terry-cloth slipper, the kind she wouldn't be caught dead in outside the house.

"A shame," Ora says. "I was thinking I'd get to see her. I always like to see Miz Foster, but you come in." I follow her through the porch, where the plastic screens are torn and flapping. A humid wind blows through the cracks; flies buzz indolently above my head in a halo of motion. I smell mildew and must and automatically breathe shallowly, anxious to get inside. The living room hosts two chairs, easy chairs draped in white sheets with an end table in between. Above us a tiny Jesus slumps on a peeling gold cross beside a curtained door. The room has little furniture, only a couch, a TV, and two chairs, all lined up in a row, facing the sagging porch. I look out the door at the empty fields, at the hazy sun and blazing strip of road, imagining hordes of mosquitoes rising out of the ditch at dusk, floating in waves toward this house, vigilant as bombers; revulsion shudders inside me and I look quickly at Ora's face, but she's gazing beyond me at Jesus, whose head bows down toward his bloody chest.

Then she sniffs, blows her nose on a white paper napkin. "Aller-gies," she says, stuffing the napkin into her pocket. "It's this heat make you sick."

I nod, feeling the sweat trickle down my collar as we talk about the usual things, about the weather and family, flying through the daili-ness of the present until there's a lull in the conversation, when im-pulsively I ask how she came to work for us in the late fifties. I can still see Ora getting out of our car, hefting up that sack of leftovers while we turn around in her dirt drive, leaving her in the sweltering heat while we race back to our air-conditioned house with its wood floors and carpets, its chandeliers and antiques, its washing machine and dishwasher, all the comforts of middle-class life. Glancing up, I notice a cheap chandelier hanging cheerfully in this desolate room, its plastic prisms cascading in a waterfall of yellow light, sprinkling the floor with patterns that shift when a sudden gust of wind breezes through the flapping plastic of the screens. It's one of the ugliest chandeliers I've ever seen.

"That's a long story," Ora says, following my gaze. She stares at me with hooded eyes, and for a split second I think she's reading my mind, and I'm ashamed that I've come here as much out of curiosity as friendship, but then her face softens as she knots and unknots her hands, worrying her paper napkin. "I can't remember things like I used to." She closes her eyes as if she's thinking about where her mind has gone, where all that stuff really does go. "But I'll try to tell you, Pat. Yes, there's some things I can tell you. You was just a girl, you know, when I come to work for Miz Foster, but it starts before that. It starts . . . well, I guess it starts after my divorce, when I had to choose between the bottle and Jesus."

The bottle or Jesus. I lean forward, staring into the stillness of the air like a little girl waiting for a story. A fly buzzes against the screen door, fluttering its wings, as Ora begins telling me about her divorce, how afraid she was, afraid of being alone, afraid of raising her two girls, afraid of not having enough money, afraid of all the heart pain of leaving her husband. "After I left him, I had me a hard time, Pat." Ora looks at me with silent knowing and I nod, thinking of my own divorce, how crazy I was, ricocheting from room to room, quaaludes squeezed tight in one hand, a bottle of tequila in the other as I drifted through my shadowless world. I try to imagine Ora in her early thirties, alone in a shack with two little girls, but my imagination falters, for in my mind she's ageless, always sitting in the backseat of our car. I look up at the ugly chandelier and see a bare bulb, fly speckled, dangling from the ceiling, or maybe a paper shade covering its rawness.

"I didn't drink much," Ora continues, shifting her gaze and looking at me with sudden gravity, "maybe a beer or two every now and then. But I *liked* it, you know. And sometimes I went to this colored club in Mobile where you could dance and drink. I'd go there and *forget*." She frowns, sucks in her breath, sends out a little whistling sigh. "This one Saturday night I sat with my friend, had me some beer, and I started telling him my worries. Told him how the beer just eased my troubles, and he looked quick at me and said just as solemn as you please, 'Well now, Ora, you can go out on weekends and drink all you want, but come Monday morning your troubles be on your doorstep just waiting for you.'"

Ora pauses, glancing up at Jesus on the cross. "And that just made sense."

I want to look at Jesus, wondering if he's happy for such a convert, but Ora holds my attention, saying insistently, "I didn't know if I could make it, Pat, 'cause the bottle can be awfully sweet. But I said to myself, 'You gotta give Jesus a chance.'" Again I nod, for I know the psychology of choosing Jesus over the bottle is the choice of self-preservation in a small southern town that depends on "good women" to bring up their children and "do right." Black women weren't exempt from such customs, their lives as scrutinized as white women's. *I'm not going to help you with that car loan if you're still hanging around with Luster Hadley. Now, he's no good and you know he's no good! He's just feeding off you, doing what you know isn't right.* If black women didn't "behave," they wouldn't find work, wouldn't be given the extra little privileges a white employer might bestow.

"And Jesus took me in," Ora nods. "He did."

For a moment I grow quiet, sad. Everyone, I imagine, comes eventually to this crossroads, this split in life where the choices are elemental, primal, downright hard. I see myself at age twenty-four after my divorce, slipping a quaalude in my mouth, waiting for the dreamy softness of surrender, my mind sap-sweet with hope, my body's tension drifting above me, scattering like dandelion fluff in the air. I'd waltz around the kitchen in my pajamas, getting a little dizzy, every-thing blurring to romantic confusion, my body as light as a feather. I'd linger at the stove. Why, it looked *wonderful,* the shiny aluminum eyes locked behind each black-barred grill, the illuminated clock a brilliant emerald green, the nicks on the dials as bumpy as braille. Why hadn't I noticed that before? It amazed me that the world could feel so good when inside I was locked in a shameful battle with myself.

"Jesus said come home," Ora whispers, staring not at me but through me, as if she's seeing into the beyond, where desires come un-raveled and lie loose and sweaty as old clothes.

I sink back into myself. Unlike Ora, I didn't wake up that fast, didn't hear anything that "just made sense," but when the quaaludes finally wore off, I too had a choice: to lie down or keep going, to follow the old life or begin a new one. But there was no Jesus to save me, no choir group singing sweet gospels in my ear; in the segregated South, Jesus redeemed the poor, the afflicted, the disinherited, while the middle and upper classes sought salvation through ambition, affairs, another round of education. Instead of religion, I chose education with its sanction of upward mobility and intellectualization, the only tran-scendence I believed in.

Ora pauses, still staring beyond me, smiling with another memory. "And it was a few years later that I came to work for your mama." She taps my hand and I'm startled back to the present. "Remember?"

And as suddenly I'm that nine-year-old girl again, moving to our newly built house, racing from room to room, sitting on all three of the toilets in the new bathrooms with a burst of pride (we'd never had more than two), then watching Mother rush around the house, talk-ing with gardeners and seamstresses and plumbers, measuring the paisley armchair, the width of the sofa for Mrs. Mayberry, the uphol-sterer who'll come with her carload of cats to pick up the material. Mother was always in motion and we were right behind her, trying to claim her attention. "*Mo-ther!*" we'd yell, running down the long hall-way, anxious and excited, until she appeared at the doorway, a pile of clean clothes in her arms. "What?" she'd ask, but immediately she was distracted, the phone ringing, the doorbell chiming, until we simply followed her around.

"What I always remember about your mama," Ora continues, still holding my gaze, "is that she never scolded you children. Never raised her voice or said no harsh word, and that made an impression on me." Ora sighs, glancing up at the pictures of Ernestine and Willomena in grammar school, their faces close together in family pictures. Willomena, I know, has recently died of cancer, but as a little girl she worked with her sister in the fields, picking beans and cotton, earning money for clothes and books, while my sister and I rode our bikes around the neighborhood, read books, and took lessons in swimming, music, and tennis. I never once thought about earning money as a child. Perhaps it's absurd to make this comparison between our lives, but it's the only way I can see the emergence of a southern identity, which was always a class identity, always a secret bullying by the haves of the have nots to accept their lot as individual and self-determined, never cultural and political. "A hard worker" was the only praise black people ever got, rarely a pay raise, only a compliment denoting willful self-sacrifice. We were raised not to *see* black people, not to think of them as people but as shadows, servants, laborers with no interior lives. The interior lives were ours. *We* felt tragedy and joy, *we* burst into the kitchen in a rage because our clothes weren't ready or our feelings were hurt, but Ora kept her feelings hidden behind silent eyes, masks of duty. Whatever emotions she had were kept from us. As for black children, they were invisible to the white community, cloaked by the apartheid of segregated schools and churches. I never saw Ernestine or Willomena except when they peeked out the door when we brought Ora home. "Bye-bye," I'd sometimes wave to their darting shadows behind the screen.

"I wanted to be like that," Ora says bluntly, staring not at me but just beyond me to where Jesus hangs on the wall, "I wanted to be like Miz Foster, but seems like I had the *tension* in me when I got home from work, a pressure I carried with me all the time." Ora is frowning now, her face knotted with remembering as if she's trying to diagnose just what that pressure really was. "It's like I just didn't have no more energy to be nice."

I think of Ora walking into her kitchen, where there's a busted screen, tree roaches scurrying through the widened mesh, their hard brown shells glittering in the overhead light. Flies buzz above the sink and gnats swim in shallow pools of light. I try to imagine Ora fixing supper, washing dishes, washing clothes in the sink, knowing the next day will be just like this one. All my life I've been taught to worship the future, to dream about tomorrow, with its bright lights and possibility, never to be pessimistic, never to assume that failure or difficulty might prevail. Education and self-discipline, I was taught, opened the road to success, but in the fifties and sixties success wasn't an equal opportunity endeavor.

As if Ora can read my thoughts, she says, "They didn't hire us at the factories or the sheds around here." She's looking again at her hands, which are work worn and wrinkled, the knuckles knotted with arthritis. "So all we had was maid work. Course, we only made four dollars a day, and it wasn't much, even back then."

I have the sudden disquieting image of those four dollars laid out on the bed while Ora stares intently at them, trying to figure out how to make four dollars a day, twenty dollars a week, eighty dollars a month, equal rent, food, clothing, heat, and medical bills for three people. Forget about Christmas, Easter, birthdays, roast beef, movies, and a hairdo. But what I see instead of the money is the Christmas dress I bought when I was sixteen, how the gold *peau de soie* fabric was tucked in tiny pleats over the bodice, giving my breasts the added "lift," how the skirt flounced out from the waist, hemmed just a little bit shorter than the other girls' dresses. "Why don't you buy a cheaper dress and give the money to Ora?" I imagine someone asking. Now my mouth goes dry as I think how quickly I might have protested, "But I *love* this dress!"

"Though I didn't make much money, I made sure my girls always had something to eat," Ora says, sounding as prideful as my mother, who often said she'd do anything—clean toilets and scrub floors all day long—for her children, but being white and middle class, she never had to. "I never let them go to bed hungry no matter how poor we was, and when there wasn't enough to eat, I just prayed one of them left me some scraps." Ora smiles, a flash of white teeth, and leans forward. "You know, I was always a praying person, Pat, and usually they left me a little bit." I laugh too at Ora's joke, aware that I've never gone to bed hungry, never had to pray for food, but as quickly Ora's face turns serious, her mouth set in a determined way. "You know, Pat, everything I have come from these two hands." She looks down at her hands, then her head snaps up and I see a strident victory blooming in her face. "These two hands."

It's the tone of her voice that startles me, makes me glance away, staring into the hazy light as if a veil has been lifted from my eyes. *Why, Ora sounds just like my mother.* They both have "the tension," both have indentured themselves to the next generation, professing no bitterness over their lot, tough, brooding women, relentless in their sacrifice. Is it because they're products of a more stoical generation, one that depended on Jesus and community to air its grievances, rather than activists and therapists? Did they learn early not to expect gratification other than for a job well done, no matter how menial? Did they agree to sacrifice everything for good children? I don't know. Maybe I'll never know. But what I realize is that my mother and Ora might have changed places had their skin color been different. My mother escaped poverty in a small mining town in northern Alabama by going to college on a scholarship at age sixteen. Education and a white skin saved her from a dreary life in a mining camp, but had fate been different, Ora might have had the same possibility.

Again, I glance up at the chandelier, trying to imagine Ora buying it, wondering if it gives her pleasure: The gold fixture beams brightly, shiny in its cheapness. I remember the day Mother bought our chandelier, the one that hangs in the dining room with crystal prisms and ropes of crystal chains, elegant and baroque in its aesthetic complexity. While the workmen put it up, Mother stood inside the door, frown lines furrowing her forehead until it was fully in place, swaying gracefully over the dining room table, set with Royal Worcester china, St. Louis crystal, and pale linen napkins.

Then I imagine Ora standing on a kitchen chair on some hazeless, almost airless day, her firm hands screwing in the tiny bolts, fingers caressing the falling crystals. Sneaking looks at Ora's chandelier, I see both women tense and anxious for this symbol of "the good life," and I can't help but wonder if it gave either of them a moment of joy. I try to imagine Ora smiling with pleasure, but what I see is Ora coming out of our house in her white maid's uniform, her face private, opaque, unreadable, and instead, I ask what I really want to know. "Were you angry back then?"

Ora's expression doesn't change, but she sits straighter in her chair, her legs sticking out of her skirt like brown stalks, veined and knobby. She clears her throat, sniffs, takes out her paper napkin. "You know, Pat, during segregation there was lots of things we couldn't do. Lots of things I didn't imagine doing. But one thing that got to me was the way we couldn't eat inside a restaurant. Now that bothered me. There was this place Bill's, and they had a window where the colored could come by and order food and take it home. But I never stopped at that window. I told myself, 'If I can't go in, then my money won't go in.'"

Ora smiles at this, and I smile with her. "Good for you," I say, but what do I really know about such courage? I've never been denied food, shelter, or medical attention, never had to "be careful" of my tone and bearing, never had to do more than rage and fret over the indignities of my life.

"But I felt hate too," Ora says, frowning, her mouth tight, her eyes darkening. "During the bad times of integration, white boys used to come through here at night shooting their guns. All we could do was turn out the lights and sit in the dark, waiting. We knew we weren't going to get no help. Who could we call?" She looks at me with a quick, penetrating gaze and I nod. "One night some boys come by and we heard them yelling and shooting. Must have had some old car because it rattled and squeaked when they stopped. I'd parked my car in the drive like I always do, and I heard that car stop somewhere outside. I'd turned out all the lamps and I just sat in my chair, holding my rifle in my lap. It was kinda heavy, but that night it felt light as a spoon. I heard them talking, you know, then rip-rip, a shot goes off—*like to scared me to death!*—then sounds like something breaking, smashing against the car, so I pointed my rifle at the door." Ora stops and sniffs into her napkin. "I could hear them laughing, Pat. I didn't know what to do, didn't know if they'd try to get in. I'd never shot that rifle before . . ." Ora shakes her head, "and there I was just waiting for what would happen next. Seems like I could hear the moon turn over. Sure could hear the faucet drip." She smiles. "Finally, I hear that old car start up, rattle, rattle, rattle, but I didn't dare move. I didn't turn on no lights. Almost forgot to breathe. Just sat there a good long time. When I could breathe right I stepped out on my porch, saw they'd shot off my side mirror. I looked at it all broken on the ground and that did something to me. I lifted my rifle and fired straight up at the sky."

Heat swirls around us and I see a spider making its slow crawl up the corner wall. Little fans of dust twirl in the air as a white Oldsmobile speeds down the road, then vanishes around the corner. The evangelist sings, *"Hallelujah! . . . God is goooood . . . he is soooo goooood."*

Hate. That word sits uncomfortably at the bottom of my spine.

It's 1968 and I'm walking along the Mississippi River, holding hands with my new husband, looking at the wild, surging water, gray-brown and fast moving, the tugboats passing under the Memphis–West Memphis bridge. We've just gotten married, are settling down to night classes and work, and I'm surprised when he pauses on the patchy bank, looking down at the grassy slopes, saying sudden, stinging words that stop my heart. "My parents got a letter," he mumbles, "from someone in your town." There's a stutter to his voice, a tightening of his mouth. He looks frightened, uneasy, and relaxes his grip on my hand. "He said I shouldn't marry you. Probably some crank"—his eyes widen in boyish concern—"he didn't give a name."

"What?" My voice rises up into empty air, the life force sucked out of me as I drop his hand to clutch my own. A storm of weeping shakes me, and I crouch to the ground, my brain bristling, screaming, then darkening inside. Who could hate me so much he'd write an anonymous note, branding me as unfit for marriage? And why? What had I done? Was it because I was moody and quiet, not cheerful and optimistic like a well-bred southern girl? Was it because I wore short skirts and hot pants like the models in *Mademoiselle?* Was it because I resisted the requirements of my class—to be gracious and subordinate, insisting that others go first while I lingered in the shadows? I stare into my open hands, feel the simmer of violence creep into my palms, and in that instant all wholeness shatters. The only thing I know is that I'm hated, and this knowledge changes me, shows me how arbitrary approval is, how—regardless of my conduct—someone in the world will find me repulsive, despicable, unworthy. Now I'll spend my life trying to pull together the fragments, covering up the raw spots, using all my psychic energy to protect myself, building an external shell, hard and resistant, to cover up the softness.

I've been pushed to the river . . .

I don't look at my husband but stare out at the Mississippi, knowing its secret, deadly currents can pull a body deep into the water, holding it fast against its mud-soiled bottom.

Though I remember this incident as a turning point in my life, undeserved cruelty was an anomaly for me, while for Ora it wove its threads through the scratchy fabric of her life. She was denied the basic courtesy of human decency, the right of agency. That's a torment I can't hold firm in my imagination, though as a child I used to wonder, "How can Ora stand it?" Now, as an adult, I know that human beings are amazingly resilient and can stand almost anything, though the mental and psychological exhaustion takes its toll. Rejection becomes a "tension" sucking hope and desire out of your skull, leaving only the dry ashes of duty. Duty, I think, can't heal souls.

"Do you hate the South?" I ask, knowing that Ora also worked in New Jersey and Michigan and Ohio, places where the politics of race were more liberal than in Alabama. Earlier in the day Ora told me about going to Teaneck, New Jersey—"way up there!"—for a year as a live-in maid with her own room in the family house, then going to Michigan to pick cherries and apples. "They treated me good," she said, "in both places. Treated me like a white person."

But now she surprises me. "I always come back to Alabama," she says, looking out the window at the fading sun and empty fields, where glimmers of light torch the dying weeds. "It was something inside me, I guess. Something that kept me. I was from here and I said to myself it ain't what the place do for you, but what you do for the place."

And I smile, pleased at what she's said, pleased that she prefers the South, as I do, not because it's a better place (in so many ways, it's absurdly anachronistic) but because it feeds something primal, a longing, maybe, that's inarticulate and necessary, the way sleep is necessary. Or perhaps it's only *longing* I understand. I think of the day in 1995 when I stood at the bend in the Magnolia River to watch the stillness of the water beneath a new growth of banana trees. It could have been 1955—the enduring silence of the place, fall leaves floating on the surface of the water like the open petals of flowers, a few boats docked under rusty tin sheds. Weeds grew up next to the shore. The air smelled of pine needles and mold. But most important, no one was around, only an occasional car thundering across the bridge, then roaring out of sight. Silence. A flight of birds. I'd forgotten the porousness of the soil, the ant beds that clung like smushed hats to the sides of trees and spilled voluptuously onto the ground. I'd forgotten the oaks and pines and palms all crowded together on a bed of soft pine needles. I stared at the river, breathing in the quiet. And for a moment I forgot myself.

And yet I didn't come to this love easily. For years I couldn't decide if I wanted to claim the South, to be southern, to try to untangle its knotted ideas about race and class. During my twenties, I hated its political and social conservatism, obstinately resented its parentage, longing only to get away, to be free of its lineage. When I left at age twenty-six, I imagined myself saying, "I'm *from* here, but not *of* here." And always I've asked myself what the South has created in me, whether that creation is a monster or a blessing, or something suspicious in between.

Perhaps every question has its moment, its season in the sun. Mine came not on that first visit to Ora but almost a year later in early spring, when the harsh weather of Iowa sends me scrambling once again to Alabama. In Iowa I walk haltingly through the snow, looking up at the bare, frosted trees into a hazy sky, longing for a golden sun. When I arrive in Alabama, leaves are sprouting, flowers blooming, grass turning a luxuriant shade of green. I throw my backpack on the sofa of my parents' house and go outdoors, finally able to breathe deeply, to feel the comfort of soft air. That afternoon I call Ora, asking if I can visit.

"Come on," she says once again. "My great-granddaughter's living with me now and I pick her up every day after school. Then I be here."

We set a time for later in the afternoon when Ora will be home, and I rush off to another appointment, a visit with my old music teacher, Mama Dot, who's just had a pig valve put in her heart. She's ailing and wants to talk, so we sit in her sun-drenched living room with the baby grand and the sprouts of cotton near the fireplace, taking up where we left off years ago. When I try to leave, Mama Dot starts another interesting story, keeping me pinned to my seat, intrigued and yet anxious. I want to hear what she has to say, but I also have to meet Ora. When I finally pull my car from her driveway, the air's turned gummy, thick, the sky a gray blanket of clouds. As I race down Highway 98—the AC on high—I know it'll take me twenty-five minutes to get to Miller's Corner, but this isn't my only worry; I've borrowed my mother's car and she hates being stranded, so I decide to check in with her before I rush to Ora's. I'll call Ora from Mother's house, telling her why I'm late, hoping she'll still have time to see me.

But the signals are already crossed, the path split, the day once crisp turning limp and stale. When I arrive at home, my parents are furious at each other—my father huffed and muttering in the den, my mother silent and seething as she strings celery in the kitchen. Coming into the midst of their boiling energy, I forget to call Ora. When I remember, it's five in the afternoon and I get the buzz of a busy signal. That night, trying again, the line crackles with static.

It isn't until I'm at home in Iowa City that I talk to Ora. It's a dark, bitterly cold evening and I'm wrapped in several sweaters, my feet in socks and fluffy slippers. I dial slowly. When Ora answers, I apologize profusely, describing what happened, my rush home and the family argument. But we both know four days have lapsed between that afternoon and this call.

Ora allows it—I can hear her soft breathing on the other end of the line—then subtly scolds me, telling me how she went early that day to pick up her great-granddaughter just so she'd be there when I arrived. "For our meeting."

I look out into the darkness, where shadowy branches wave stiffly in the howling wind, and feel ashamed, guilty, thinking, *This is written into our history, this caste system of black and white, and I've unwittingly obeyed its rules.* But, of course, it's more than that.

Later that night as I huddle beneath the blankets, I wonder if Ora had been someone of my own class, my own race, would I have behaved differently: gone by, if only to say I couldn't stay? Made a more conscientious effort? Called sooner? Behind rudeness, there's always hierarchy . . . it's just a matter of stripping the behavior down to its roots. And I know that in white culture Ora is expendable; she's not worth interrupting a family crisis for. No matter which way I cut it, my own rudeness indicts me, aligns me with my dominant culture, which says that Ora doesn't count, isn't a part of me, is just a woman who sits in the backseat of our car. For years I've told myself that I'm different from other southerners, liberated from my past, but what if I'm not? Can I ever talk to Ora about this, not just about the racism but the "classism" of our lives, the way even the style and value of a chandelier separates us? I shake my head, knowing that this is the conflict I'll never lose, this sense of myself as caught between two worlds, unable to speak.

As I'm fretting about this, I hear a loud crash as if something has exploded just outside my window. I sit up, heart hammering, excited but waiting for disaster. And yet when I lift the curtains to peer out, I realize it's only an avalanche of snow falling from my roof, thundering to the ground. I sigh with relief and snuggle back in bed, staring at the silvery moon frozen in a winter sky. But oddly, the metaphor holds: being southern I've often felt this same lurch of disaster, the surge of love and guilt crashing through my psyche, startling me to attention, waking me to a quivering rage. In the midst of this anguish, my heart seizes up, opens, and empties, my nerves buzz like high-tension wires. Just as I see the slit in the universe, I'm already falling, bathed in a blistering light. Maybe, for me, that's all the South will ever be: an emotional jolt, an arc of feeling, a racehorse in my blood. I've thought for a long time that I'd simply grow old and die trying to figure it out, but lately I've come to see that this ambivalence *is* my southern identity.

I walk amazed beneath a curtain of green: oaks and pines and Japanese magnolias. To my right the waves of Mobile Bay drift lazily toward shore, their white foam ruffles like the lace of a petticoat. Seagulls cry as they fly overhead, dipping suddenly as if dropped from a string, searching for food. To my left a row of two-story Creole houses with fern-decked porches blossom in sea blues, pinks, and greens, their white picket fences, draped with bougainvillea and wisteria, face streets named Freedom and Liberty. A banana tree sprouts new bunches of bananas; a ripe bloom hangs limp, purple as a plum beneath its clusters. Drunk on beauty, I'm caught in my own fantasy land of place.

And yet this is the town of my birth: Fairhope, Alabama. Surely back in 1948 it was little more than an eccentric village on Mobile Bay with a nominal postwar economy, dependent on farming and fishing, hardly worth notice except for its socialist past in the early 1900s. Now it is, quite simply, something else: a Gold Coast, a hatching ground for Protestant wealth as the equestrian classes take a frantic leap across the bay in pursuit of better schools and fewer minorities, joined by coupon-clipping retirees moving down from "up north" (Michigan, Wisconsin, Ohio, Pennsylvania), with their Lincoln Continentals, their flat, ironed syllables, their Dole/Kemp bumper stickers. But it's this *something else* I'm curious about, for in my childhood, Fairhope had the feel of a quiet, bohemian village of artists and craftsmen, farmers and businessmen, who thrived on this untended garden by the sea. Now the garden is being tended; Eden is harvesting money, acquiring an aristocratic veneer, a kind of internal colonization where what was good (land by the sea) is being bought and refined and in its refinement excluding me from its secret life.

I have come walking this morning to take my own temperature about place, to try to understand my feelings of loss. I pause to stare at the new promenade of maple trees and flowering plums, the beds of pansies and geraniums blooming along Main Street, the stores brightly painted, their windows dark shuttered and quaint like stores in the older districts of New Orleans. It's true that Fairhope is more beautiful than ever, and yet, as I glimpse glossy, well-tended ferns, blood-red carnations wooing me from window boxes, I feel sick, as if I have a low-grade fever. Although I've read numerous novels about the American zeal for wealth and status, it's never touched my life so uniquely, never occurred in my own backyard. As a child I came here for dancing lessons at Miss Roberta's, music lessons with Mama Dot, and spend-the-night parties with Susie Blachford. I went horseback riding and sailing, slept on beaches, waking clammy and chilled to the fusty smell of the sea, only to rush out to the pier to feed the seagulls, their cries so primal they sent shivers up my spine. Now the beaches are full of tourists, the streets glutted with overdressed shoppers, with lawyers and financial advisers in three-piece suits, toting briefcases and computers; to my horror, it's a place where all the women are thin, all the flowers are in bloom, and all the men make big money.

What has happened to the place I once knew?

I can't begin to tell you this until I sketch for you the place I once loved.

I am eleven. I wake to early morning light, to hard white sand and a sea shimmering like glass. Seagulls glide toward the pier, their great wings flapping. All around me are sleeping bodies, kids tucked into blankets and beach towels, bodies huddled around the long-dead fire, the girl next to me whispering, "I found it! I found it!" in her dreams. This is the first time I've ever slept on the beach, the first time I've awakened so happy I want to jump out of my skin. There's sand everywhere: in my hair, my underpants, caked under my fingernails, squished between my toes. But today I don't care. Today nothing matters because I'm lying on cool sand with my music class and Mama Dot, my music teacher, who insisted we celebrate our summer recital with an overnight trip to the beach. I wouldn't be here if this wasn't Fairhope, a place where our creative life spills easily into sensual pleasure, where it's okay to be eccentric, okay for men to weave blankets and women to carve statues, okay for everyone to read newspapers from the big northern cities, okay to eat eggs with big clumps of sand stuck to the plate.

I look over at Claire, who's turned away from me in sleep. She's skinny and freckled and noisy. She wears baggy shorts and ragged shirts the color of lint, something I'd never do. Most of the time she's either bossy or distracted, except when she's playing music and her mind's turned inward, her body completely still, her gray-blue eyes half-closed as if she's dreaming. She's like the other Fairhope kids, the ones who go to Organic School, who come to Mama Dot, who act as if they can make themselves up, starting from the inside and working their way out.

Before breakfast we all rush into the water, which is cool and brackish, the tide so far out we walk a half-mile in shallow water before it's up to our waists and we can play underwater tag. When Claire pushes me under, I let myself settle on the bottom, the silt rising, swirling around me, hiding me from the world. When I'm tagged, I come up quickly for air. I see Mama Dot moving toward us in her funny brown bathing suit, the bottom half like shorts, the top a crisscrossed halter, her boobs drooping inside. Claire splashes her, a thick wave of water that slaps against her shoulder and face, and with sudden relish, Mama Dot splashes her back.

I laugh, then dive back underwater, pleased that this odd crew of kids, artist kids with stringy hair and crooked teeth, may be the only world I need to know.

At the center of this world is Mama Dot, a woman who has such odd ideas she astonishes me. For one thing, she never wears dresses.

"Now, what would I do in a dress?" she asks, looking up at me as she bends in her garden and mulches the tomatoes. Unlike my mother, she likes to squat in the dirt. All year she wears wrinkled khaki shorts or pants and faded knit shirts or sweaters and ugly orthopedic shoes from which her long, thin legs emerge like stalks. When she's restless, she pushes her thick pelt of short hair back with her fingers and stares out the window at the deep green monkey grass growing alongside her brick walk. And yet with all of this unfashionable weight, she's incredibly beautiful, not in the typical southern way of soft voluptuousness but in the clarity of her bones, in the clear gray of her eyes, in the ease of her movement when she leans forward while listening to Beethoven or Brahms. Though, like our mothers, she spends time in the kitchen, she doesn't cook the same kind of foods. She uses "organic" foods, a powdery flour that's not quite white, and lots of vegetables I've never heard of: beet greens and acorn squash, Swiss chard and brussels sprouts, when canned peas and corn are popular.

But more important than this, Mama Dot insists on originality. No longer will we perform in stiff, formal recitals where we wear our best dresses and play a single piece of memorized music. "That's silly. It's more fun having recitals in my living room," she says, putting pillows on the floor. And it's here that we play several pieces for an audience of mothers and sisters (only occasionally fathers), sometimes duets and trios, and once, I dance—like a ballerina on a music box—on top of the piano. I remember the day Mama Dot suggested it. I thought she was kidding when she put down the lid on the grand piano and said, "Climb up." She began playing a movement from Mozart, leaning into the piano. "Make up a dance to this," she said and closed her eyes.

"I can't move," I said from my perch on the piano. "There's no space."

"Good," she said. "That will teach you compression."

Two times a week Mama Dot sits beside the piano while I play Grieg, McDowell, Shubert, Bach. "Again," she says, staring at me with silent intensity, and for a moment I imagine us walking together through the desert, the heat a halo of energy cradling my head. I close my eyes and play soft, soft, then fast as if my fingers are pushed by a night wind. I want to play well, to be accomplished, and yet secretly I know it's not music I learn at Mama Dot's but the pleasure of the natural world. When I'm not having a music lesson, I often ride bareback through the woods with Geoffrey, one of Mama Dot's sons. He's tall and handsome, a junior in high school. I'm thrilled that he even knows who I am. Often we keep the horses at a walk, following a familiar path, the trees above us shading us from the sun. One bright summer day with no clouds, nothing but enduring blueness, we emerge from the woods by a farm where cows graze and an old red barn sits on a small rise full of wildflowers. My horse feels huge, his coat stiff and bristly beneath my thighs, my hands clutching his dark shaggy mane. He suddenly gets frisky. "Midnight wants to gallop," Geoffrey says. "You think you can handle that?"

I've galloped with a saddle, riding with Geoffrey after my music lessons, but I've never galloped bareback. I'm a little frightened, but I say yes.

And then, almost before I can catch my breath, we're flying across the farmer's fields. Or the closest thing to flying I've ever done.

When we arrive back at Mama Dot's, I'm flushed with excitement. She's just finished my sister's lesson and she smiles as she hands me a washcloth and towel to clean up. "I bet that was fun," she says, believing that fresh air and animals are as important as music and dancing in the scheme of things. It's this perspective I associate with Fairhope, the belief that every part of life is serious, passionate, that wherever you fix your gaze is where you are.

As a child I'm ignorant of Fairhope's history, unaware that its founders were Iowa socialists who moved to the Deep South, then built a town based on the philosophy of Henry George, a single-tax colony holding land as community property, certain that the evils of society came from owning and exploiting land. It was a utopian system known as "cooperative individualism," which meant that almost all property except land was privately owned. Right behind the single-taxers came the Organic Education movement, a school started by Marietta Johnson, who told educators and parents all over the United States that "it was the whole child" that must be attended to, that the child need not be exploited by acquisition, grades, ratings, or adult expectations. Instead, the child, like the earth, was resonant, a bedrock of abundance and desire, encouraged to follow her curiosities, to squat in the dirt and study bugs, to sing, to fret over the mysteries of human nature. I remember being jealous that students at Organic often held classes outdoors, planned their own curriculum, and learned folk dancing and art at the end of each day rather than once a week. Of course, not all the students were southern, since the warm climate and reformist philosophy were so agreeable to many Yankees that they boarded their children at Organic School, then traveled to Europe to spas and resorts.

"Uncle Kenny was raised by Marietta Johnson," Mama Dot tells me, her voice reverent, as we walk through the tall grass of her backyard to the cottages Uncle Kenny is building. The cottages are small brick houses in a glade of grass and azaleas, with monkey grass paths leading to a stand of pines. I hear the whine of the saw, the stutter of hammers. "I used to practice at the school, and sometimes Aunt Mettie [Marietta Johnson] would call the other kids into assembly to hear me play. Uncle Kenny always grumbled, 'Dorothy's having an A-seembly,' because it cut off his recess." Mama Dot smiles. "But it was good for him. After we married he finally learned to like Mozart."

We push through bushes, Mama Dot parting them with her hips. She stops to pull a thorn from the hem of her shorts, then picks up her narrative. "Aunt Mettie absolutely *saved* him, brought him up and gave him a home and showed him the importance of working with his hands." She looks beyond me to the mimosas in bloom, trees full of delicate pink parasols hanging upside down. "He has this wonderful mechanical sense, but without her, he might have just sunk."

I see Uncle Kenny squatting on the roof, his skin tanned, his crew cut like the bristles of a hairbrush. He doesn't notice us, so we watch as he fits another tile onto the roof, then stands up quickly, tottering there with nothing to hold on to but air. For a moment Mama Dot goes still. "He's okay," she says, then moves on past the azaleas. Uncle Kenny, I think, was saved for Mama Dot.

Three or four times a week we go to music and dancing lessons in Fairhope, driving down the Greeno Road, a two-lane blacktop with soybean fields on either side, each curve, each barn memorized, tallied as if we're involved in a formal dance. Sometimes we stop at old Mr. Barnum's farm and pick up bags of pecans, the trees planted in precise rows, the branches shading us like summer umbrellas. We put our feet on the bags as we pass trailers hiked up on concrete blocks, graveyards sprinkled with plastic roses, shallow rivers, tin sheds, solemn cows grazing in the fields. Other times we stop at Mrs. Ingersholl's house, where Mother drops off medicine for a foster child with "im-pa-*ti*-go," a word I love to say. The drive is a series of "moments" until we turn off into the curving street that is Fairhope, our car dipping into a hollow of cooler air where another life begins, the life of the senses. Cinnamon, sea, the sounds of Chopin.

Thirty-three years later I come back to Fairhope, to a place where humanistic reform and financial boosterism inevitably collide. No longer is this a sleepy southern town with "lots of interesting folks doing some unusual things" but a town where the price of land is outrageous, where high-priced boutiques sell T-shirts beaded with the hood ornament of Mercedes Benz, where most of the artists and the working class have moved out into the county because rents in town are "impossible." Million-dollar homes sit behind guarded gates, extravagant houses facing sea and light, silhouetting a bruised blue sky. Where women once discussed "the vote" in grocery stores and town meetings, today they gab about cruises and debutante balls and plastic surgery as they shop in stores where cut flowers are sent out to be "freshened." Nobody wears wrinkled shorts. Everyone's hair looks nice. The retirees seem completely free of arthritis. I walk around town bewildered, slightly ashamed that I look so ordinary.

This week I will help chaperone my nephew's end-of-school party, a private school just outside of Fairhope in an adjoining wealthy community known as Montrose. I know the party will try my soul in a way that children in groups of ten or more always do. This, of course, has nothing to do with my nephew, whom I adore, but with the fact that I will probably not fit in with the well-heeled Republican parents, the New Royalists, who now rule the once socialist Fairhope.

As I get ready for bed the night before the party, I mentally prepare myself for the inevitable class warfare. I know that I'll be attentively ignored by most of the mothers, solicited for pouring Cokes and 7-Ups for children, checked out with that once-over gaze that leaves me suddenly aware of my absence of a hairdo. I don't have to look in the mirror to see that my nails are chipped, bitten to the quick, that my skin is fish-belly white. I have not shaved my legs in weeks—or is it months?—and I don't wear mascara. I look, I think, like a woman in a hurry, a woman with other things on her mind. If I didn't know better I'd think my appearance would be simpatico with the other mothers, for I've always assumed that mothers are allowed to look disheveled. But from another year, I know these women will come to the fourth-grade party in five-hundred-dollar shorts outfits or sundresses, their hair highlighted, cut for a quick shake of the head, their tans even and smooth. "It's a Versace," one of them will say about a see-through silk blouse. "I picked it up in Italy last summer." Even their toenails will be painted a delicate frosty peach. They wear earrings and matching sandals, and when I look at them I think, *Jesus, you're a far cry from Mama Dot.*

But here goes. I put on jeans and a T-shirt, lace up my tennis shoes, and with my nephew in tow, drive to Fairhope. We go for miles through a lush canopy of overhanging limbs, the Spanish moss dripping from the branches. Beyond the bank of trees, Mobile Bay stretches before us, waves rippling slightly, the sun a white oyster hanging limp in the sky. There's such simple elegance in the land that my spirit relaxes, softens. Even though I've been away for many years, the physical beauty seduces me, calms me into a less critical stance. I want suddenly to be here, to get out of my car and run through the trees down the sandy dirt road to the water as I used to with Mama Dot. My legs ache with this desire as the curvy road twists around trees and houses, the bay visible, then hidden, visible, then hidden. By the time we find the house where the party will be held, I'm in a lighter mood, not exactly hopeful, but one step closer to optimism.

We park under the shade of an oak tree, and I have no sooner gotten out of the car, picked up the beach towels my nephew has left on the backseat, than I see the replica of a black slave jockey that stood in the yards of plantation society. He is grinning, holding one hand out, ready to hold the reins of the guests' horses. It's only a moment, but seeing this antique I know that this will be a group of white children, their awareness of race and class potentially obscured by the similarity of their backgrounds, of trips to Europe, to the Caymens, to Alaska, to Greece. After all, this is a private school, the training ground for the next ruling class, and I know enough about culture to understand that the main task of the New Royalists is to legislate themselves, to restrict membership. Me? I'm an interloper, an intruder in their midst.

As I'd expected, I'm not warmly welcomed, though after the first impersonal scan, I'm simply ignored as an innocuous guest with frizzy hair and baggy jeans. The women introduced to me are well groomed and youthful, and the children, much to my delight, are curious and hungry for adventure, as healthy children usually are. Although nothing of particular significance happens at this party—the children play games, swim, eat, have accidents, take risks—the event makes me think more deeply about the details of class expression and the underlying difference the wealthy have made in a community like Fairhope.

What first comes to mind is my own caution, the way I become self-conscious, all spontaneity drained away as if suddenly I'm irrelevant, invisible. I find myself staring into windows, silver trays, a woman's sunglasses, trying to fathom how I look. *Do I look okay? Am I still here?* And, of course, I try to imagine what these women feel about me as I help their kids line up at the diving board. I suspect it's merely detachment, nothing so human as active dislike. But no matter, for I'm busy fetching towels, watching my nephew, putting mayonnaise and mustard and NO LETTUCE on his hamburger.

When I go to the kitchen to scoop up a bucket of ice for the kids, a woman beside me is pouring iced tea. She glances at me sideways. "What do you write about?" she asks, squeezing lemon into her glass.

I'm startled by her question and wonder how she knows I'm a writer. "I'm writing a book about the female body."

"Oh," she says as if perplexed. Then she makes a face. "I don't want to know another *thing* about my body."

I nod, mute, unable to respond, then glide smoothly outside to stare at the bay, forgetting all about the ice. While standing on the pier I remember reading about the early suffragists of Fairhope, women who worked hard for the vote, who believed in a woman's voice as utterly necessary to social reform. As Marie Howland, one Fairhope woman, put it in 1912, "I have long known that the cause of woman is the cause of the world." I've thought of these early feminists as my ancestors, my lineage, and I've adopted Fairhope, preferring it to my own hometown, where German and Czechoslovakian farmwives worried about getting meals on the table, keeping kids in school, canning vegetables, making clothes. They baked strudels and braided coffee cakes and fed the hired hands; they wrung chickens' necks, gathered honey, made wine. With such work they probably had no time and perhaps no inclination for social policy. I imagine when they looked out their windows at night they didn't see women demanding their piece of the pie, but the flat expanse of potato fields, the star-hooded sky, and a man still riding a tractor.

As I stare out at the bay, at the sky where the sun rolls up its sleeve and gets busy, I know I secretly believed I'd grow up to claim Fairhope as my own, that I'd do something dramatic in the world, then come back to live gracefully beside Mobile Bay. I saw myself slipping into this place as comfortably as into an old shoe, this place that would keep me awake and amused, satisfied with myself. But now I see that this isn't true. I'll never come back. I'll never fill that hole of unquenchable desire. And though I don't want to turn over this card, to stare at the naked truth, I see that in the eyes of the New Royalists, I'm a risk, a failure: no savings, still renting.

As I drive my nephew home, a great weariness descends as if I've trekked through difficult terrain, swampy ditches with snakes and alligators, places where danger is as vivid in speculation as in reality. But once I'm back in my hometown, I look out at the fields, the straggly pines, the hog wire fences, and find the beginning of a quiet affection.

Maybe wishing that Fairhope had stayed the same is an act of nostalgia, the way you miss not the events of childhood but its essence: the hum of crickets, the sputter of a motor somewhere out in the bay, wet bathing suits, the snapping of crabs inside a rickety crab trap, and the silent suddenness of a pale moon rising through the dark thickness of night. I loved it there, even the bugs that crawled into Mama Dot's house, hard shelled and ambitious, or the garden snake that lay on the porch, moving from the scrub grass and pines into the warmth of a sun-drenched floor. No doubt the houses are better insulated today. Surely the air conditioning silences the sounds of crickets and the fidgeting of the crabs. Thinking this, I wait sullenly for night, for darkness, for the etched light of the moon. When I walk outside, it is full and luminous, rising through its own nocturnal duty, ceaseless, silent, unaware that Fairhope has been bought.

As I pay my respects to the night, I remember a tall, white-haired man who once visited Mama Dot. She asked him to stand up and recite a poem. "Oh, do it, Pete," she begged. "Do the one about the hobo." Pete smiled shyly, looking down at his large feet. When he raised his head, he spoke softly, reciting the life of a boy who jumped freights, who traveled alone, moving into the deep purple night of the West. His voice was slow, melodious, full of deep sorrow. I knew immediately that he was the hobo of the poem, and it astounded me that here was a man who had lit out for the territories, who had chucked security, home, and family, living only on raw need. You can do that, I thought, as if someone had opened a secret door. You can go away and come back and write about it. You can risk falling in love. You can risk flailing in despair. In the end, that's what Fairhope meant to me: It gave me permission to live by the heat of my nerves.

EPILOGUE

WHAT PLANET ARE YOU FROM? _____

We begin in early morning darkness. A cluster of stars in a black night sky, the air soft, clinging, wet against my skin. No one is on the road except truckers and fishermen and the three of us gliding down a two-lane blacktop, the woods thickening around us as we leave behind the flickering lights of small towns. I ride in sleepy silence with two men and a boat hitched to the back of the truck. We're headed for the Tensaw Delta, this wide fist of a river that opens its fingers to the Apalachee, Blakeley, and Tensaw rivers, smoothing its palm into the easy lap of Mobile Bay. Now, in gray dawn, there's only wilderness, heavily wooded land, a latticed darkness, interrupted by occasional houses and beat-up trailers and old cemeteries gone to weeds and brambles.

Much of the land around the Delta, the men tell me, has been bought up by the state as a nature conservatory. "Used to be no-man's land full of gator poachers and child molesters," Mike says, glancing out the window at the dark outline of the trees, "but now they're Republicans and bankers."

As the sky lightens, a pink thread through the blanket of gray, I ask how gator poaching works.

"You mean how do you *kill* a gator?"

"Yeah."

"Well, you gotta remember trying to find a gator brain is like trying to find a Republican brain," Mike, a staunch Democrat, says, "so it can't be that hard." He laughs at his own cynicism, then explains how the poachers use several methods, none too sophisticated. "Sometimes they bait a big hook with spoiled meat, luring the gator, and once he's hooked, well, they shoot him right between the eyes. Easy does it."

Later when I see one of those scary things, I'll think twice about how easy this could be: The gator swims stealthily through the water, camouflaged in color, only eyes and snout hovering above the surface. Once it sees us it submerges quickly, gliding backward, descending into the depths like a submarine. To be a gator poacher, I decide, you've got to have a lot more testosterone than you need.

There's barely a halo of light at the horizon when we pass Bushy's Landing, then pull in to Live Oak Landing, a graveled driveway that curves between oaks and cypress trees and ambles down to the water. All along the landing, boat lights blink in the darkness.

"Damn bass fishermen," Luke says.

"Good Lord," Mike agrees. "Look at 'em."

"What's wrong with bass fishermen?" I ask innocently, having never met such a creature in my life.

"Well, Jesus, look at them all huddled there together. Like a bunch of nuns. Never go anywhere but in a pack."

"And all because of these damn bass tournaments," Luke says.

"Bass tournaments?" I ask from the backseat. I live in the middle of the middle of the country, where the only bass I ever think about are the kind I order from a menu.

Both men stop talking and stare at me. "What planet are you from?" Mike asks, because clearly I'm not from theirs.

I sink back into myself as if I've been scolded, but then something flares up in me, rises defiantly. I'm from the planet of women. The planet of insight and clarity, the planet of uncomfortable shoes, bright lipstick, and good table manners. First, I should tell you that I'm not a sportswoman. I've never put a worm on a hook, never shot a gun (much less killed a deer), never been scuba diving or snow skiing. I'm no daredevil, have had no desire to jump out of an airplane or drive a car at ridiculous speeds. I like simple things: sitting in the swing on my front porch, riding safely inside a well-stocked boat, having a picnic in some bucolic place where there are butterflies and gnats, but no mosquitoes and bees. I'm of the generation of women who worried about entering the public world, about making careers and becoming financially independent. Though I've wanted adventures, those adventures have centered on traveling to foreign countries, experiencing the diversity of culture, learning to say hello, how are you, and where's the bathroom? in Italian and Greek. It would never have occurred to me in my twenties and thirties that a trip down the Delta, this place in my own backyard, or at least in the backyard of my childhood, would be an adventure, something that would teach me about myself.

"Bass tournaments," I say now, "are as foreign to me as men on the moon."

Mike spits out the window. "Don't you ever look at Discovery Channel?"

I don't. I don't know anything about lures or traps or poachers or the habits of southern men. I grew up in the little toe of Alabama, surrounded by creeks and canals and swampland, but I left in my twenties and have come back only for short visits to sit in my mother's kitchen.

Bass tournaments, the men explain, are Saturday entertainment for southern men who come from all over the state to work the rivers. And I see it's true: They're here at five this morning, their boats lined up in the water like cars in a Kmart parking lot.

"And here's another one," Mike says as we watch a red truck, a boat hitched to the back, bounce toward us. "That's a cowboy Cadillac for sure," he says, though it looks like every other truck I've seen. "See, it's got a rebel flag on the license with a bass on it."

"Republican," Luke says. "Count on it."

As we enter the water, I think immediately of the movie *Deliverance,* of that trip the Atlanta businessmen made down the Cahulawassee River. I'm as innocent as they were, as naive about the way of the river, and more to the point, about the people who live on its shores. Mike and Luke tell me lots of gang rapes and wife killings take place in these parts because it's an isolated, lawless place. I want to be shocked because these are the words of thriller stories, of shock fiction, but they're both lawyers who have represented almost every kind of felon in the county, and I suspect what they say is true. Automatically, I check out the seated figures of the bass fishermen, but to my eyes, they look absolutely normal.

We've come here to get a quick peek at the beauty of the Delta, to see up close the endless lacing of cutbacks and creeks, the jutting fingers of cypress trees, knees up as if they're hitching posts, Spanish moss trailing just above the waterline. A filmy mist rises from the center of the river. On the bank a heron arches its willowy neck. I've come here also to hang out in male territory, to see if men really do what male characters in southern fiction suggest: not just drink and fight, but seek solitude and companionship on the river.

At first I don't see the fishing camps sprinkled along the river's edge, floating houseboats where men must live alone. I say this because they look like the worst kind of housing, mildewed, moldy, seedy-looking containers. I can't imagine a woman living in one, can't imagine the funky dampness, the dirt, the constant whine of mosquitoes, the threat of water moccasins and alligators, not to mention cotton mouths and eels. Even as I sit comfortably on the boat, I imagine the toilet in those riverboats, how they must stink of human waste, but also of the rot of the river, the inevitable decay of nature. I turn my face instead toward the wide-open channel of water, often forty-seven to fifty feet deep, the wind brisk and cool in my face on this early August morning. I feel fated to be here, fated to be a listening presence to these men, since I've spent all my life with women, often indoors and sheltered, a book in my lap. Today the river is our living room, our dining room, our den.

The men, like the men in Larry Brown's *Fay*, don't say a word about their personal lives, have no impulse to gossip or reveal their innermost thoughts. Instead, we watch the shore like people looking at TV, attentive, engrossed, studying it for any curiosity, any signal of nature: herons, egrets, brown pelicans, moccasins, gators. When a pelican lands on an unlikely tree, its branches spindly and bare, we applaud. "Would you look at that?" Mike says. "Can you imagine hanging on to that little bitty branch with those webbed feet?" It's a brown pelican, a species that was almost extinct but now is flourishing. All around us cypress trees and oaks bend lazily toward the water. Moss hangs down like old men's beards. All around us the woods encroach on the river while the river wears away at the shore.

We drift first into Mifflin Lake and Squirrel Bayou, then head down the Tensaw, cut through the gas line canal (which was dredged to lay pipe) to Big Lizard Creek, which twists in curvy female fashion into Little Lizard Creek. In Little Lizard Creek we see the papa gator, an eight-footer, blind in one eye, its red orb cobwebbed with filmy whiteness. "That's why he's letting us get so near," Mike says as he cuts the engine. At first only his reptilian head shows above the water, a prehistoric head with bulging eyes. He's swimming close to the bank around an old cypress tree, and we float toward him. I see now the dreaded girth of his body beneath the water. The sheer length of him makes me shiver. Normally, he'll "go under," as we say, but because we're on his blind side, he doesn't seem aware of us. Then, as suddenly, he is. He vanishes, sinking backward as if he never existed. A ghost.

"That son of a bitch was BIG," Luke says, and I'm relieved the gator has left us, that despite my quest to "see the Delta," I don't have to contend with its ugliness.

As we meander through the serpentine twists of the river, I think about what the men have told me. *This is a place where people disappear, where men come until their warrants run out.* And I can see the advantage. You could get lost here. You could lose yourself. You could hide out in some fishing camp and no one would know you were there. All along our route we see abandoned fishing camps, the stilts of these one-room huts standing beneath a tangle of vines. Sometimes the tin roof has slid to the ground, held up by rotting boards. Other times the camp is almost intact, the rough walls buckling, the windows broken out, the porch an avalanche of split wood. Each is tucked neatly into the woods, always built on stilts, with wooden walkways to the pier. All look forlorn, sinister, and yet I can imagine a man hiding here, fishing every morning, hunting deer and quail during the season, drinking in the afternoon, going to the local landing once a month for supplies. As long as solitude wasn't a problem, you could wait out whatever trouble dogged you in the real world. You could get good and lost.

Back at Live Oak Landing we see two "old boys" fishing from the pier. They look as lifeless as two wrung out rags. "They're on sabbatical," Mike says, chuckling.

"Too many footnotes to finish on their dissertations," I say.

"Yeah, who wants to spend all your time quoting sources," Luke says. "When you can fish."

Another man, more sinister, one who could audition as the evil antagonist in a Hollywood movie, stares at us from another pier as we pull the boat up onto the trailer. His eyes are hooded, alert. He watches us as if we've invaded his territory, as if we're trespassing on sacred ground.

"Howdy," Mike says. But he doesn't respond.

"I wouldn't mess with that one," Luke whispers. "He's been up here too long."

It's only as we're driving away that I realize I haven't seen another woman all day. But it makes sense. This is a man's world. A place they've claimed for centuries.

Early dusk. The sky is pale blue, dusted with clouds as if they've been finger-painted across the heavens. The air is mild, moist, but the oppressive heat of midday has lifted and a light breeze comes off the bay. Tonight I'm going out frog gigging and gator shining with Ray, a silver-haired man with the rough, weathered skin of an outdoorsman and a reticent gentleness that makes me soften, begin to feel at ease. I've spent the better part of two days trying to cancel this trip, then being persuaded to "hang in there," as Mike and Luke say, because what's an adventure without a little fear? When I want to cancel, I think about the darkness of the night—"can't even see your own damn hand," I've been told—and about the fact of being out in the bayous and marshes in a small boat with a man I don't know. What I do know is that there will be plenty of gators and mosquitoes, possibly snakes and nutria rats to contend with. Not to mention the frogs. What I do know is my own intolerance for fear. What I also know is my willing seduction to strange beauty and the risk of adventure. Like the heroine in a novel, I'm pulled both ways, wanting danger and safety, risk and caution, surprise and order. I'm my own ridiculous contradiction.

"Oh, go on," Mike says, badgering me, hands on his hips. He rolls his eyes and shakes his head in disgust. "What could possibly happen out there except for snakes falling in the boat and a coupla gator sightings. Now don't tell me you're not up for that."

"It's just not enough," I say.

"Well, you haven't figured in the mosquitoes." Eyebrows raised.

I think of the recent press on West Nile virus, how seven people have died in Louisiana, and of the mosquito spraying I see each night on the highways.

"'Sides, there's no moon tonight," Luke says. "It'll be slick dark out there, and there's the noise of all those bullfrogs to get excited about."

"Yeah, that's a turn-on."

"There you go. What's not to love?"

But at three in the afternoon, I'm tired and grumpy and have plenty of reasons to say no. I think of mosquito bites lacing arms and legs or, worse, some reaction to the DEET these men spray on like cologne. It took me thirty minutes to wash the DEET out of my hair yesterday. I see myself terrified and stuck out in the middle of nowhere with nothing but terror for company. I'm absolutely committed to my "no" and tell them it's all off. Over and out.

And yet to my surprise, I'm quietly disappointed in myself, in the inevitability of "no." At four a compromise is found. Margaret, a young woman just back from a year abroad, says she'll go with me. "She's great. She'll do anything," Luke says, letting me know she's not the traditional stay-at-home southern girl. And suddenly everything seems clear though nothing has really changed. It's simply a matter of sharing the danger.

We set out from Mozell's Fishing Camp near Mobile in a little fiberglass boat —not much bigger than a pirouette—with an old motor and two paddles. Life jackets are stashed under the seats, never worn. We do a run down the Apalachee River, the boat bucking the current, striding the middle of the river. On each side the banks are thick with trees and brush, but here on the river there's nothing for miles around but dark blue water. It's oddly exhilarating. I have a moment of such intense pleasure I think nothing can touch me. Nothing can happen to me. As long as we're running the river, I'm invincible.

"Heading for the Mudhole," Ray tells us. Just south of Blakeley, he slows the engine to enter a slough, a serpentine canal that winds through the marsh, a hidden hallway between the Tensaw and the Apalachee, a kind of winding cul-de-sac, one of those places where enough silt has settled to support the vegetation. The water here is as smooth as glass, as reflective as a mirror, and I can't help but think of myself as Katherine Hepburn on the *African Queen. I raise an imaginary umbrella and press a scented handkerchief to my temple.* We could be on that movie set in Africa with miles of bamboo and lily pads, with wild Queen Ann's lace and lime green saw grass. There are no trees, nothing higher than the shoots of bamboo; most of the vegetation is as benign as the lilies that grow wild here, everything lush and green. "This is it," Ray says. "The Mudhole." When we cut the motor and drift, we hear the groans of the bullfrogs, low, rough croaks, then a soft pop as they swallow air. Dragonflies buzz just above the lilies and the mosquitoes whine incessantly.

Because we must wait until dark to gig frogs, Ray, Margaret, and I entertain ourselves, letting the boat drift into the lily pads and nudge into bamboo. Ray tells us how the marsh wasn't always here, that in the forties the state brought in nutria rats for the fur trade, but not only the trade but the rats flourished, eating everything, even the marsh grass, so that none of the sloughs existed. "It was barren," he tells us. "But then they got them under control and the swamp came back."

In the fading light of dusk, the slough is beautiful, a silvery sheen on the water, the air like velvet. I'm thinking how easy this is, how absurd to have been afraid, when Ray says to Margaret, "Of course, there are gators here. They're out there right now."

"Ooooh, I wish I could see them," Margaret says wistfully.

"I'm glad I can't," I say.

"You will," Ray says.

But for another hour I don't have to.

And then suddenly, it's dark. Not just evening, but pitch black with only a thin slice of moon and a flicker of Venus to light the slough. What was beautiful before has quickly become ominous, but before I have time to worry, Ray straps a light onto his hat and shines it into the marsh. We're seriously looking for frogs now, and he starts the motor, guiding us slowly through the slough, casting the light at the banks, scanning the lily pads on which frogs like to perch. The long gig is held to one side of the boat, and though we hear the chorus of frogs we don't see many. We see gator eyes—lots of them—red bulging eyes riding the surface of the water. They don't move when the light hits them, but inevitably Margaret calls out "Gator." Ray tells about catching three gators about two feet long. "Brought them to my daughter's party to tease the boys. I just caught them with my hands," he says. But I don't want to hear any more. I want to concentrate on the frogs, such benign creatures, so I shine my light back and forth across the banks, though I see no "eyes." My own eyes aren't trained for such observations, and I'm surprised when both Ray and Margaret see them easily.

"You know I have panic attacks," I tell Ray, though it's not really true, merely my excuse for not staying out all night on the river. I tell Ray one or two hours of frog gigging is probably enough for me.

"Whatever makes you comfortable," he says. And I believe him. I don't think he'd do anything that would make me anxious, though I know he can't understand my fears. To him, the river is like his back lawn, as temperate and benign as a grassy yard. He's already told us that four years ago he had cancer: He opened up the collar of his shirt to show us the diminished size of his neck, said the chemotherapy and radiation nearly killed him. "It changed me," he said. "I didn't want all the hassle anymore. I'd been a contractor for years and when I came home I was always tensed up, so I'd go out on the river for a couple of hours and come back as calm as you please."

When we find frogs, Ray tries to gig them, but it's a cumbersome process because he has to manage the motor and the gigging, whereas usually he has someone else to handle the motor. Now he must deftly cut the engine and ease to the front of the boat (never losing the frog in his light) while lifting the gig. He lunges, but the frog jumps easily into the tangled darkness. Disappeared. He tries again and again, almost succeeding. I can tell he's disappointed, but as we spot the twelfth and then the fifteenth gator, I wonder if his disappointment is equal to my fear. My heart beats rapidly. I pull my arms tighter around my body, trying not to shiver. Surrounded by gators, I feel the river is oppressive, and I want to go back to the landing.

"Okay," Ray says. "But lets go back through another slough on the other side."

"Sure," I say, though what I want is to be riding the river, speeding over that rough current in the dark because it's too deep there for gators and I don't know what creatures might lurk beneath. Instead, we speed through the narrow tunnel-like canal of the second slough, coming out at a wider area, a place where there are more gators than before. They're like traffic cops on a busy corner. Every time we shine the light, there's another one. Suddenly Margaret wants to catch one—"Oh, could we plleeease!" she begs. She's terribly excited about it, and to my surprise, Ray heads toward the bamboo as if he wants to satisfy her. He slows only when he hears the croaking of the frogs. We go silent, still, the night closing around us, the whine of mosquitoes filling my ears. Ray raises the gig, angles . . . but it's no good. Sighing, he turns off his light and starts the motor.

It's cool now and the darkness cloaks us. We head into the main channel of the Apalachee, and as we ride the river, I feel lighthearted, generous. I wish I could say, "Go back, Ray. Let's all go back and find those frogs." But I don't.

Instead, I talk to another man, Bruce, about the gators. "At night, it's like New York City out there," he says, staring at me from under his ball cap. "All them eyes."

I nod. That's what it felt like to me too, and I wonder if Bruce has ever been to New York City. He's lived in Bay Minette, Alabama, all of his life and worked at a factory here for twenty years. "Have you ever been to New York City?"

"No," he says, grinning. "Just as far as Baltimore, but you get the picture."

Bruce has been going frog gigging since he was ten, when he went with his dad. Now he goes with his buddies in an airboat, a "sleek little honey with a big airplane propeller," which gives them an advantage because they can lie on the deck of the boat and grab the frogs, gigging them only when they're tucked deep in the grass. The airboats can ride over the top of the grass, can get into places a small boat can't. And when the men go, they make a night of it, leaving at nine when it's full dark and staying until six-thirty the next morning, packing in an ice chest of beer, some food, cold drinks . . . "just about anything you want to take."

As a female tourist in this land, I can't imagine what they do for so many hours. Gigging frogs, for me, has a three-hour limit, but these guys are lifers. And besides, they like to "play with the gators," which means they shine their lights on them, then grab them just behind the neck "same as you would a frog," Bruce says, "and lift them out of the water so they're mighty confused." Bruce tells me they do this only with the small ones, the three-footers, not anything much bigger, though he's seen gators seventeen feet long, five feet wide, *the big guys*, the kind you want to imagine only in the movies. "We go when the moon's waning, the tide low. Then it's too dark for them to see you. You've got the advantage."

I'm trying to understand where the thrill is, what the river gives to these men. And it is mainly men who seem obsessed with the river, not just with fishing and frog gigging and gator shining, but with the preservation of a place, with keeping it "as it is." When we ran the river this week, it was the mist rising off the water, a soft veil of fog drifting toward the banks, that moved me. And yet what I felt seemed contradictory, inexplicable: A profound sense of my own insignificance washed over me while alongside it came a heightened alertness that left me breathless. I had no defenses, no armor. Whatever was malevolent or destructive in the river could disarm me, destroy me. The hairs on my arms stood up. My knees tightened. And yet, simultaneously, I couldn't stop staring at the velvet green lily pads, fluted, flat, spread out like elegant dinner plates. All my senses were awakened to the unnamed beauty as if nature had opened up her hidden hand.

"River Prozac," Bruce says. "That's what it is. You go out there and everything's just better."

As I go to bed that night I think about the planet I'm from, the world of women, wondering about our differences. The women I know drink as much as the men, take on as much work and as much worry, live the bulk of their lives not in the kitchen but out in the public world, making a living. And yet the conversation's different. The stories turn not on "the biggest fish you ever saw" or "last year's hunting season" but on figuring out how to get along with your mother, keeping your kids out of trouble, or finding a moment alone to read a good book. On the planet I'm from, risk is more likely to be emotional and intellectual rather than physical and communal, and the rituals of to-getherness most often combine child care with pleasure or sneaking out to the back fence for a smoke so the kids won't know. No women I know get up at four to meet at Mozell's Fishing Camp or spend all night out on the Tensaw gigging frogs. No women I know get antsy right before hunting season, though I know women who hunt and always have. I'm sure there are such women. I just don't know them. They're not part of the legacy of my generation.

Drifting toward sleep, I think about how glad I am that the world of men and the world of women still have nuances of difference. I think of the lingering silence on the river, the men quiet, attentive, the smell of DEET and dampness in the air, then the sudden rush of talk as my mother and sister come to tell me news of my niece's new baby. I like that there is plenty of danger and silence in both worlds and that to cross the boundaries is no longer a transgression, neither an act of power nor of powerlessness, but a choice. I like that I'm most firmly wedded to the world of women, that intimacy is bound to the interior world, that emotion is the catalyst for ideas, and children hold first allegiance. But I would be foolish to deny my pleasure in the river, in that world where men have always come to be meditative and still.

When I close my eyes, I see those giant lily pads of the Tensaw Delta, the lilies like white fists, as fecund as if they might burst. Some already had. The pods resembled alien eyes: puffy-dark, foreign, forbidding. And I'm reminded that where there's beauty there's danger, and that danger in its natural form is alive with beauty. I knit that thought in my mind as I smooth the covers and press my cheek into the pillow, thinking of the wild canaries Mike said sometimes nest on the river. In that moment I see them: a burst of whiteness, the ghostly flutter of wings, their sounds surreal, melodic, otherworldly as they fly over the foggy skin of the Delta.